A Pictorial History of H.S. Chase Elementary School

Compiled by Michael Griffin

Printed in the United States of America

First Printing, 2022

ISBN: 979-8-218-00508-5

Cover photos contributed by Lori Anton-Ritch, Ivan Hernandez, the Waterbury Board of Education and the Gottscho-Schleisner collection at the Library of Congress

Highbury Press
P.O. Box 3447
Waterbury, CT 06705-3447

www.highburypress.com

CONTENTS

INTRODUCTION

This book has been composed in observance of H.S. Chase elementary school's centennial year, with 2022 marking 100 years since the oldest sections of the current site were built and the school was named in honor of Henry Sabin Chase.

While 1922 was the year that construction began on a new school building, the history of the school and district on the eastern side of Waterbury go much further back in time.

The following pages present a journey through that history, dating back to when the area was known as the Saw Mill Plain section of Waterbury – and one of its fourteen school districts – in the mid-1800s.

The city's development into a center of manufacturing by the 1900s led to a boost in population, requiring a growing need to enlarge the school system to accommodate the increases in enrolled students.

Expansions of Mill Plain School (later named H.S. Chase School) helped meet those needs, and the school continues to serve residents in the East End of Waterbury. While no longer a full K-8 school, Chase's history serves as a reflection of a broader school system adapting to changing times.

As a former student at Chase, it has been a joy to search through microfilm archives of old newspapers, Board of Education reports and municipal registers to gain historical information for this book. Assistance has also been provided by research staffers at the Silas Bronson Library and Mattatuck Museum, along with contributions from a number of people with the Chase Centennial and Waterbury East Enders groups on Facebook.

I hope that this helps to bring back some memories for readers!

– *Michael Griffin*

Source: Waterbury Board of Education's 1904-05 Annual Report

Architect Joseph Smith's drawing of Mill Plain School, part of plan proposals submitted to the Waterbury Board of Education in July 1904 for the construction of a new building for the district.

ORIGINS OF THE SAW MILL PLAIN SCHOOL DISTRICT

The history of schooling in Waterbury dates back more than 300 years. The first reference to schools in town records comes in 1698, although "it is probable that a school, taught by the younger Jeremiah Peck, had been established fully ten years before that date," according to Joseph Anderson in his "The town and city of Waterbury, Connecticut" history.

No public school of a higher grade than a "common" or "district" school existed in Waterbury through much of the next century – as private institutions were more prominent – until an academy near the Green was founded by Reverend Joseph Badger in 1784.

Ecclesiastical societies had managed education-related affairs throughout Connecticut communities for much of the 1700s, before the General Assembly in 1794 formed school societies that were empowered to levy a school tax, employ a tax collector and build school houses. The state sold its Western Reserve lands the next year, with proceeds from the sale helping to finance school operations for years as the public school system began to develop in state municipalities.

The School Society of Waterbury emerged as the local agency, but early records of the society were destroyed in a fire in 1833. That same year, a school house was built in the Saw Mill Plain section of Waterbury, according to the history of Mill Plain Union Church – which conducted its first services at the school house. Maps of the time, including the one shown

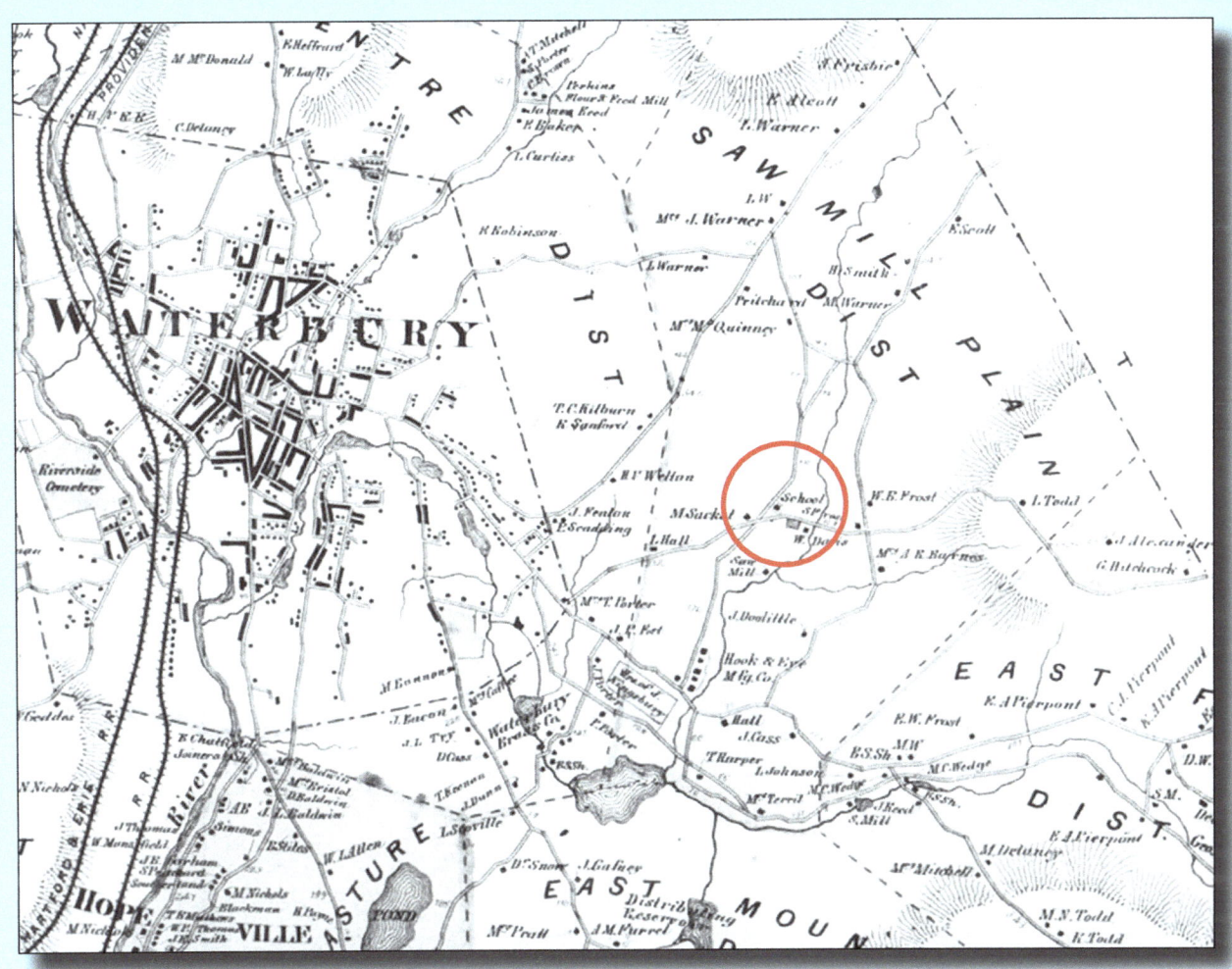

Source: Homer Babbidge Library at UConn

The school house for the Saw Mill Plain district can be located in the circled area on this map, dating to be from 1874, showing magisterial districts and residences in various regions of Waterbury, from the Petersen Collection at the Map and Geographic Information Center in the Homer Babbidge Library at the University of Connecticut.

above, show a school located a short distance further up Woodtick Road than the current site of H.S. Chase School.

By the mid-1800s, the society had divided the jurisdiction into fourteen school districts, consisting of a central district along with a ring

A home located a few hundred yards from the current Chase School, on the opposite side of Woodtick Rd., sits on the site of what was the Saw Mill Plain school house in the 1800s.

of outer districts within Waterbury's boundaries. Districts in the eastern fringes included Saw Mill Plain, so named because of one of the first saw mills that operated in the area.

In 1853, the year that the borough of Waterbury was officially incorporated as a city – a vote enabled school officials to oversee "the purchase of the following sites: a lot on Grove Street at $500; a lot on Mill Plain, corner of Elm and the street that runs to the cotton-gin factory, $800; and a lot on the Prospect road, $500. On some of these lots, but not all, school houses were built," according to Joseph Anderson's "The Town and City of Waterbury, Connecticut."

(It is believed that the "Elm Street" in that note may have been the current Meriden Road, with the "cotton gin" considered to be the property that would become the Mattatuck Manufacturing site.)

By the time a general state statute was passed in 1860, free schooling had already been made available by law in Waterbury. The School Society held authority over all educational concerns within Waterbury's Centre District, while combining with committees in each outside district to oversee affairs in those locales.

"Wrangling over control of the city's schools was lessened in 1899 with creation of the Department of Education and a controlling board made up of the mayor (ex-officio) and seven members (to be selected to be selected biennially at the regular municipal elections)," as noted in "Waterbury: A Pictorial History" by the Mattatuck Historical Society.

The School Society era thus came to an end in the final year of the century, with Waterbury in the midst of a period of tremendous growth in population – caused by the successive waves of European immigrants to the area and the city's expansion as a major industrial center.

"Two years later, the way was opened for the (outlying) school districts to amalgate with the city system," according to the historical society's account, "but not until 1915 did the first district (Town Plot) decide to take this step." The Mill Plain district voted to join in 1916.

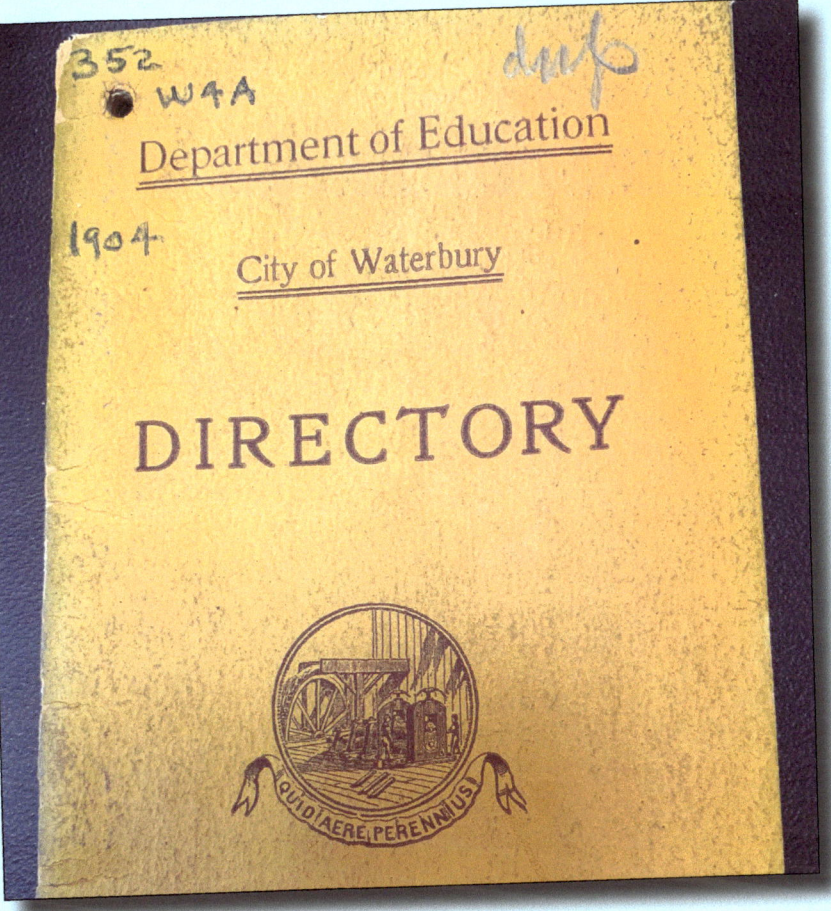

Department of Education

City of Waterbury

DIRECTORY

QUID AERE PERENNIUS

352
W4A   dup

1904

SCHOOL ENROLLMENT FROM 1867–1901

Year	Enrollment
1867	2800
1882	3700
1887	4178
1892	5462
1894	6047
1901	8913

HOPEVILLE SCHOOL
Cornel Chapel Street and Pearl Lake Road.
Fanella E. Peck, Principal.

ROOM		GRADE	APP'D
4	Fanella E. Peck, 61 Chapel Street......... 7		1900
3	Minnie A. Norton, 85 Ridgewood St....6 and 5		1903
2	Carrie H. Clark, 84 Chapel Street......4 and 3		1901
1	Marjorie C. Rigney, 39 Hawkins Street..2 and 1		1903

MILL PLAIN SCHOOL
Woodtick Road.
F. May Tatem, Principal.

ROOM		GRADE	APP'D
4	Elizabeth Ives, R. F. D. No. 1.........7 and 8		1903
3	Clara Marshall, R. F. D. No. 1.......5 and 6		1903
2	May Kershaw, R. F. D. No. 1.........4 and 3		1904
1	F. May Tatem, R. F. D. No. 1.........2 and 1		1894

NEWTON HEIGHTS SCHOOL

ROOM		GRADE	APP'D
	Susie S. Chambers, 118 Cherry Street....Mixed		1899

ORONOKE SCHOOL

ROOM		GRADE	APP'D
	Margaret C. Coe, Maple Street, Waterville..	Mixed	

Source: Waterbury Department of Education's 1904 City Directory

Mill Plain School's teachers are listed among the staffs at district schools in the Waterbury Department of Education's 1904 directory (shown in graphics above).

Source: 'An Historical Study of Public Education In Waterbury, Connecticut'

The rapid increase in children of school age in Waterbury between 1867 and 1903 can be seen in the graphic at left (from Mary Lonergan Iorio's 1968 thesis project).

A NEW SCHOOL FOR A NEW CENTURY

B y the early 1900s, concerns were growing that the school house wasn't sufficient to house the growing number of students in the Mill Plain region.

In the 1903 annual report from the Waterbury Board of Education, an account on the condition of schools notes that the Mill Plain district "has outgrown its present quarters, the seventh grade being held in a neighboring hall. Some provision should be made in the immediate future for the erection of a new school, capable of meeting the needs of the present school population and ample for the future growth."

The following year, there was debate among district residents whether to add on to the school or build a new structure. At a June 1904 meeting of the Mill Plain school district, with 96 residents on hand, it was decided to abandon the idea of putting an addition to the old school and build a new school instead.

The issue remained a hot topic in the region as discussion among electors turned to the location of the new school, with some district residents satisfied with the existing site while others preferred a more level plot with less of a sloping grade.

Special meetings were held the next month, with building plans accepted at a July 9 gathering, before a crowd assembled on July 29 to decide on a location. According to the next day's report in the Waterbury Evening Democrat (shown partially at left), some attendees walked two miles to attend and cast their vote.

Waterbury Board of Education members were present to offer their opinions as well, preferring the option to change the site and

Source: Waterbury Evening Democrat

At left, parts of an article from the July 30, 1904 edition of the Waterbury Evening Democrat, about the previous night's meeting of the Mill Plain district regarding plans for a new school.

MILL PLAIN DISTRICT.

Held Interesting Meeting Last Night in Regard to School Matters.

The question of erecting a new school house and selecting a site for the same has aroused the residents of the Mill Plain district more than any other question considered by the district in many years. It has brought back old and gray haired veterans into the field of public life from which they have been missing of late. It has put new spirit into the district, for it has stirred the voters and taxpayers to attend the meetings and have a voice in the expenditure of their money.

For some weeks the district has been red hot over this school question. Many residents knew that the present school belonged to a by-gone day and desired a new one, but they were opposed by a large number. They won finally with the aid of the board of education, and then the fight over a site began. This matter was settled at an important meeting of the district last night in a room in the school building, which was lighted with two lamps and a lantern. The meeting was largely attended, many persons having walked two miles or more to be present. The meeting was rather quiet and orderly and was like a Sunday school session, compared to some meetings of the Town Plot school district.

After the meeting had been called to order by B. F. Hogart, Daniel Squires was selected as moderator. He made a good presiding officer. Charles S. Chapman, J. J. McDonald and Finton J. Phelan, representing the board of education, occupied seats of honor near the moderator's desk and were warmly applauded when introduced to the assemblage.

On behalf of the special committee, consisting of Messrs Warren, Heaton, Pritchard, Gallagher and Hogart, Mr Warren reported that it was the unanimous report of the committee that the site of the school be changed, and that the Swift lot, a part of the old Dr C. ...rt Ward property, be purchased, provided it could be purchased for $800. The lot has a frontage of 114 feet, is rather flat and is not far distant from the Mill Plain chapel.

A communication presented by Mr Heaton was read, showing that forty or more property owners were in favor of a change of site, while two signed their names as opposing it.

Mr Richards said that the present site was a fine one and better than the proposed new one. Mr Warren could not agree with him. It would cost a lot of money to get the present site into shape for a new school. Many accidents have occurred to school children on the present grounds owing to its condition, and the little children are always in danger of being injured. On the new site little grading would be needed.

William Atchinson spoke as follows: "I am pleased to-night to see that for the first time in twenty years that the members of the board of education in their capacity as school visitors are present at our meetings. We have been voting for them for years, but they never came near us. I have been twenty years in Mill Plain and this school has always been an eyesore. It will be a wise thing to move the site, for it will cost $1,000 more to build here than on a flat site. The child of a friend of mine was pushed down the bank here once and crippled for life."

At the request of the meeting the commissioners of the board of education then spoke.

Both Mr Chapman and Mr McDonald were in favor of changing the site, the present site being unsuitable because of the grade and several other reasons.

Mr Chapman also said, "We wish you to have better surroundings. At present you are not getting the worth of your money, nor is the city getting the worth of its money, and the city pays considerable toward the support of the school. The teachers have filled the bill as well as they could, but they are not doing the work they should because they have not the facilities. As a consequence the pupils when they come into the city are not up to grade and have to be kept back a year or so. All four teachers have been recommended very highly and have been given a certificate. The city stands ready to give to you anything used in a modern school house. It is also imperative that you maintain a school house while the new one is being erected."

Students at Mill Plain School, circa 1909.

agreeing with the committee's recommendation to pursue the purchase of "the Swift lot, part of the old Dr. C. Art Ward property ... provided it could be purchased for $800."

A ballot on a motion to change the site was ultimately taken, resulting in 34 out of 50 present voting in favor of a new site – just enough to secure the required two-thirds vote for passage.

Ground was broken for the new structure – at the corner of Meriden and Woodtick roads, and opposite the Mill Plain chapel – on Sept. 21, 1904.

Apart for some minor items, the new building was ready for the opening of the 1905-06 school year.

By the beginning of the 1906-07 school year, the committee in charge of the building of the new school house at Mill Plain – consisting of B. F. Hoggett, Thomas Heaton, M. A. Pond, E. S. Pritchard and J. F. Gallagher – was given a vote of thanks for its service at the district's 1906 annual meeting and officially turned the property over to the district.

MILL PLAIN SCHOOL

The new Mill Plain School building will be situated at the intersection of the Meriden and Woodtick Roads.

The building has a frontage of sixty-two feet and a depth of forty-five feet. It is planned for a four-room school house having two rooms on a floor, with a fifteen foot corridor running through the center from front to rear. Well-lighted play rooms are provided in the basement, and also a good boiler-room and compartment for coal. The building is planned so that more class rooms may be added at any time.

The class rooms have a seating capacity of forty pupils each, of the grammar grade.

The blackboards and chalk rails are the regulation heights, the blackboards being carried completely around the room wherever possible, both for convenience and to carry out the finish of the room. The style of the building is old colonial, and has a very pleasing exterior.

Open wardrobes in corridors, bookcases, teachers' closets and toilets, and principal's room are provided.

The heating and ventilation is accomplished by a gravity system, being a combination of the direct and indirect systems of radiation.

The building is well constructed and due consideration has been given the comfort and convenience of both teachers and pupils, and sufficient egress in case of fire or panic.

The building was designed by Architect Joseph T. Smith of this city.

Source: Waterbury Board of Education's 1904-05 Annual Report

A page taken from the Waterbury Board of Education's annual report for the 1904-05 school year offers a description of the new school for the Mill Plain district.

The new Margaret Croft school was occupied this fall. In point of sanitation, heating and lighting, and general arrangement for school purposes, this school should rank as the best in our City. It is a far cry from the unsanitary, unhealthful and unsafe Elm Street school to this modern building. One need not hesitate to compare this building with any similar building in this State or in New England.

DISTRICTS.

The past year has been one of great progress. There is scarcely a district but what has spent or is spending large sums to put its school property into excellent condition. I do not think that it is too much to say that at the opening of the next school year we shall have the finest district schools that there are in the State and it is a matter of congratulation to the various districts that they have provided so amply.

BUNKER HILL.

A new and more central site some 200 by 375 feet in size has been purchased and a brick school is in the process of construction. The building will contain the latest ideas on heating, ventilating, lighting and sanitation and when completed will be second to none in our City. A full description of the same is given in the last pages of this report.

BUCK'S HILL.

A new site 100 by 275 feet has been purchased and a commodious two-room building erected. The children now attending school will have a better opportunity than has been possible in this district during the past twenty-five years. A full description of this building is given in the last pages of this report.

MILL PLAIN.

The new Mill Plain school has been completed. A finer structure for school purposes or better adapted to meet the needs of any district does not exist in this City. Every citizen of this district should rightly feel that they have good reason to be proud of what they have done.

"The new Mill Plain School has been completed. A finer structure for school purposes or better adapted to meet the needs of any district does not exist in this City," proclaimed a review of district buildings within the Board of Education's annual report for 1905-06. "Every citizen of the district should rightly feel that they have good reason to be proud of what they have done."

The continued growth of Waterbury was again apparent in the school records that year. Student registrations in Waterbury totaled 9,413, an increase of 697 from the previous year.

The new school site in the Mill Plain district was among a number of construction projects within the school system. "Bucks Hill started on its new structure; Park Road opened its new four-room

MILL PLAIN SCHOOL.
Woodtick Road.
Sadie F. Rigney, Principal.

Room.	Grade.
4.a Sadie F. Rigney, 149 Cooke Street	8
Marjorie E. Warner, Assistant, 717 East Main Street.	
4.b Ethel L. Carnes, 236 Boyden Street	7
3.a Ria H. Kirjassoff, 190 Southmayd Road	6
3.b Irene M. Sullivan, 695 East Main Street	5
2.a Rose F. Kirjassoff, 190 Southmayd Road	4
2.b A. Irene Chatfield, 62 Madison Street	3
1.a Julia R. Sheil, 143 South Elm Street	2
1.b Belle Gordon, 190 Southmayd Road	1
Marie C. Schmitz, Sewing, Cheshire, Conn., R. F. D. No. 1.	

Source: Waterbury Board of Education's Annual Reports

Above, a list of the teachers and principal for the 1916-17 school year at Mill Plain School in Waterbury.

At left, a report on the year's construction in the city's school system, from the Board of Education's annual report for 1905-06, includes a glowing review of the newly-built Mill Plain School.

building. During 1904 and 1905, the districts voted over ninety-four thousand dollars for sites and school buildings," according to the "History of Waterbury and the Naugatuck Valley (Connecticut)," by William J. Pape.

These expansions came during Berlin W. Tinker's term as school superintendent. He served in the position from 1896 until 1925, a period that saw some the greatest changes in the Waterbury school system while the city's population rose from 43,000 to 108,000.

Tinker introduced many new programs and courses and saw the school system through the flu epidemic of 1917 and World War I. A number of outlying districts took advantage of the amended charter of 1901 to officially consolidate into the city's Department of Education during Tinker's term, including the Mill Plain district in 1916.

Photo contributed by Ray Sullivan

Students at Mill Plain School in 1911. Graduates that year included Mansfield Gillette, later president of Waterbury Savings Bank and a drum major of Mattatuck Drum Corps, and Jessie Aitchison Sullivan, who lived in the house shown in background at left.

CLASS DAY EXERCISES IN MANY SCHOOLS

Programmes and List of the Graduates That Have Been Prepared For Entrance to the Crosby High.

As there will be no session of the public schools to-morrow, it being circus day, the ninth grade classes held their class day exercises this afternoon. A few of the graduating classes combined their flag day programme with their class day exercises. The exercises consisted chiefly of recitations and essays. As class day is much more enjoyable to the graduates than the commencement exercises, they naturally look forward to the day, and their parents and many friends are as a rule present. This afternoon the schools were all well attended and in addition to receiving much entertainment from the programmes, found much to interest them in the exhibitions of class work.

The programmes and list of graduates of some of the ninth grades follow:

Grammar School Grade Exercises.

The Grammar school grade exercises will be held at Poli's theater on Thursday, June 18, at 2 o'clock. The public is invited to attend the exercises. No admission tickets are required by adults.

Nicholis: historian, Gertrude Pyne;

Mill Plain School Graduates.
Elby Baker, Olga Hansen, Lyndel Heaton, Ruth Lockhart, Frank Miller.

Town Plot School Graduates.
Nora Adams, Frank German, Carl Gensler, Marie Hargraves, George Hinman.

Sprague School Graduates.
James Barrett, James Burns, Harold Hubbell, Edward Meyer, Clifford Welton, Alice Chatfield, Katherine Dunn, Ida Hapeman, Mary Riordan, Lizzie Sizer.

Bunker Hill School Graduates.
Myrtle Atwater, Beth Burritt, Josephine Dawson, Ola Davis, Helen Farnham, Leslie Griswold, Ruth Jerman, Marion Keavaney, Maria Moody, Wesley Moody.

Chapel Street School Graduates.
William Baer, Ethel Davis, Eva Dulac, Lucy Dulac, Gertrude Dwyer, Minnie Henderson, Gertrude McAlenney, Helen McAlenney, Frank Norton, Dudley Pierce, Ethel Pierce, Earl Pilkington, Joseph Pilkington, Stanley Vaden.

Duggan School Graduates.

Source: Waterbury Evening Democrat

A newspaper article from June 1908 lists graduates from various grammar schools in Waterbury.

The following is the school registration for 1917:

Crosby High School	897	Slocum	581
Wilby High School	553	Sprague	473
Abbott	171	Town Plot	303
Barnard	332	Walsh	1,092
Begnal	415	Washington	585
Bishop	530	Webster	829
Bunker Hill	315	Welton	223
Columbia	266	Maloney	622
Croft	1,396	Bucks Hill	40
Driggs	800	Chapel	179
Duggan	715	East Farms	33
Hamilton	90	East Mountain	87
Hendricken	384	Hopeville	127
Merriman	583	Oronoke	16
Mill Plain	227	Park Road	47
Mulcahy	446	Reidville	107
Newton Heights	52		
Porter	230	Total	14,172
Russell	426		

Source: 'History of Waterbury and the Naugatuck Valley'

At left, student enrollment figures for the 1917-18 school year in the Waterbury school system are listed in the first volume of the 'History of Waterbury and the Naugatuck Valley,' by William J. Pape, editor of the Waterbury Republican. That year saw another increase in registrations, marked by the opening of the city's second high school and the continued expansion of district grammar schools.

Source: Waterbury Board of Education's 1916-17 Annual Report

Below, a number of improvements at Waterbury schools are listed in the city Board of Education's annual report for 1916-17. That year saw upgrades made to the grounds at Mill Plain School, along with the installation of a clock on the front of the building.

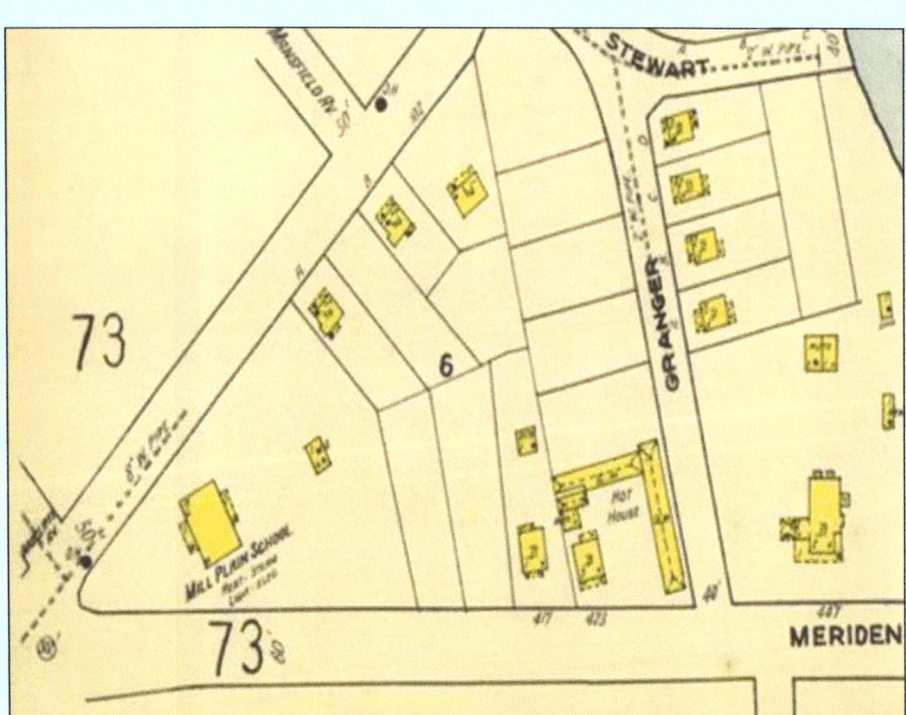

BUILDINGS AND GROUNDS.

The Hendricken School has been entirely remodeled and five rooms added.

Land has been purchased and contracts let for the new fireproof Begnal School.

Additional land has been purchased adjoining the present Crosby High School and plans prepared and contracts awarded for the erection of a large addition to cost about $500,000.

The Washington School ground has been largely increased by the purchase of land and the whole has been graded and fenced.

The Mill Plain grounds have been graded and concrete walks have been laid both within and without the same and an electric clock placed in the front of the building.

Needed trees and shrubs and hedges have been set out on all of the various school grounds.

All of the buildings are in excellent condition and a full

Source / Sanborn Insurance Co.

At left, a page of the Sanborn Insurance book of maps of Waterbury for 1921 shows the Meriden Road/Woodtick Road area with Mill Plain School included.

HENRY SABIN CHASE

Contributed / Riverside Cemetery

A marker at the gravesite of Henry Sabin Chase in Riverside Cemetery in Waterbury.

"A man of rare vision in the world of business adventure and one whose understanding heart lent cheer and courage to his fellow men. A man, he seems, of cheerful yesterdays and confident tomorrows."

— words from a plaque in Henry Sabin Chase's honor on the old Chase Companies building

In coordination with the enlargement of Mill Plain school in 1922 and 1923, the school was renamed in honor of Henry Sabin Chase, a member of a prominent Waterbury family who played a major role in the development of the group of companies bearing the name Chase, as industry began to flourish in the city in the early 1900s.

"In addition to being an industrialist, banker and lover of art, literature and nature, Henry S. Chase was concerned with public improvements, socially and aesthetically, and supported numerous beautification projects" in the region, according to his biography in Silas Bronson Library's "Waterbury Hall of Fame."

Born on October 1, 1855, Henry was the eldest son of August S. Chase – also an industrial leader as president of the Waterbury Manufacturing Company, a maker of brass products in the late 1800s.

Henry went to Waterbury schools before attending the Gunnery School and Hopkins School. He graduated with honors from Yale College in 1877.

As noted in the library's biography, Henry S. Chase succeeded to the presidency of the Waterbury Manufacturing Company after his father's death in 1896.

In 1917, "he presided over the company's merger with the Chase Rolling Mill Co. and the Chase Metal Works to form the Chase Companies. The firm became one of the global leaders of the brass industry, with 4,000 employees making some 33,000 products."

A great supporter of the aesthetic movement known as the "City Beautiful," Chase contributed to the grand architecture in downtown Waterbury by engaging noted architect Cass Gilbert to design the Chase Office building on Grand Street, which now houses municipal offices.

He died on March 4, 1918.

Contributed / WikiCommons

The Chase Building in downtown Waterbury, built as company offices in 1917.

MAJOR CHANGES IN THE EARLY 1920S

Waterbury's emergence as the brass capital of the world had helped to spark such a boost in population that the city's school system required even further expansion.

A proliferation of home building in East End neighborhoods of the city by the 1920s meant that the relatively new Mill Plain school wouldn't be equipped to handle the growing number of students and families living in the area

Thus, a large addition to the school was proposed, among the various building projects undertaken by the Department of Education that decade.

The school board's ultimate approval of construction resulted in a $200,000 project ar Mill Plain School that took place over two years – with more than $107,000 spent in 1922 and over $93,500 more spent in 1923.

The existing school was retained as a front for the new building, which extended eastward from the corner of Meriden Road and Woodtick Road.

The impressive new section wasn't the only change for Mill Plain School at that time. The city's Department of Education had begun naming new school buildings in various disricts in honor of prominent Waterburians, and selected Henry Sabin Chase as namesake for the East End school.

HENRY S. CHASE SCHOOL

Source: Waterbury Board of Education's 1924 Annual Report

The greatly expanded Mill Plain School was named for Henry S. Chase during the 1922-23 school year.

Chase, who had died four years earlier on March 4, 1918, was president of the Chase Companies and largely responsible for the firm's growth into one of the "Big 3" brass companies in the city – and the world – in the early 1900s.

The modern school was a fitting honor to Henry S. Chase. More than an industrialist who helped spur the city's growth, he was a supporter of the aesthetic movement known as the "City Beautiful" and contributed to some grand architecture in Waterbury – and the new school served as one more example of that concept.

HENRY S. CHASE SCHOOL
Corner Woodtick and Meriden Roads
Sadie F. Rigney, Principal.

Room		Grade
5.	Sadie F. Rigney, 149 Cooke St.	8
	Marjorie E. Warner, Assistant, Geography, 299 Meriden Rd.	
6.	Ethel L. Carnes, Arithmetic, 286 Boyden St.	7
7.	Helen G. Griffin, Language, 312 Wolcott St.	6
8.	Rosaline M. Bolger, 4 Dikeman St.	5
12.	Ethel P. Aitchison, 103 Woodtick Rd.	4
13.	Substitute,	3
10.	Josephine Murnane, 83 Waterville St.	2
11.	Ida R. Brown, 78 Abbott Ave.	2
4.	Grace C. Luddy, 172 South Leonard St.	1

Anne Garvey, Kindergarten, p.m.
30 John St.

Mae L. Dowling, Assistant,
45 Harper's Ferry Rd.

Elizabeth M. Whitehill, Cooking,
20 Woodlawn Ter.

Aidan J. Donahue, Woodworking,
47 Wolcott St.

Kathleen Blacker, Sewing,
30 Albion St.

32

Source: Waterbury Board of Education's 1924 Annual Report

An expanded staff (shown above) was in place for Henry S. Chase School in 1924, following a renovation project the previous two years.

The two photos at right show newly constructed rooms in the school – the kindergarten room (at top) and a classroom (below).

17

Eliminate Hazard On Meriden Road

City Moves to Have Sidewalks Erected — Recent Accidents Speed Program

Immediate steps to have sidewalks laid on Meriden road from the Henry Chase school in Mill Plain, northward, were urged last night at the meeting of the board of works as a result of the recent accidents to children which have occurred on that thoroughfare. Senator Joseph H. Lawlor, who in the last legislature succeeded in having a commission appinted to study the advisability of such walks all over the state, brought the matter to the attention of the works board, las night and following hearty endorsement by Mayor Frank Hayes, Superintendent of Streets Thomas Fleming and City Engineer Robert A. Cairns were instructed to confer immediately with the state highway department to see what can be done.

Waterbury would be willing to lay the sidewalks, even if the cost is great, Mayor Hayes declared, providing strips of land along both sides of the Meriden road are dedicated to the municipality. The road from Mill Plain, northerly, is maintained by the state of Connecticut. Condemnation proceedings, it was pointed out, would be costly but the state could give the necessary land along the sides of the pavement to the municipality.

Mayor Hayes stated, in agreeing with Senator Lawlor, that no time should be lost in laying the sidewalks. Cost, he stated, should not go into the matter when there are children's lives at stake. The entire board agreed with him and today Superintendent Fleming was expected to make contact with the state highway department and make some arrangements for a conference.

In the last session of the legislature, Senator Lawlor introduced a bill calling for the appointment of a commission to study the need of walks along state highways. This

Governor Wilbur L. Cross, recommending the construction of such walks. However, the state highway department has always been opposed to such a plan on the grounds that the expense would be too great.

Superintendent Fleming was instructed by the board to request the American Brass company to repair the roadway on Washington avenue where the tracks of the company's railroad siding cross the highway. Commissioner James A. Phelan complained of the present conditions at that point.

The board authorized Superintendent Fleming to proceed with the installation of sewers in Robert and White streets and Bonair avenue. It was voted to hold a hearing at the next meeting on the proposed layout of Platt street. This layout is only for a portion of the thoroughfare.

It was voted by the board to order sewer assessments laid on Luke street and Sylvan avenue property a few years ago collected.

Samuel Holzer asked the board to pass a vote ordering the piping of a stream that runs through his Vernon street property. The cost, though, will be about $100,000 and Mayor Hayes expressed doubt that the city could consider the undertaking in view of the fact that the stream is a natural water course and runs through private property. However, it was decided to look the situation over once more.

Maps for the layout and grade of Hallock street were ordered prepared and a petition for a layout of Hungerford avenue was referred to the street committee. A hearing was held on sewer assessments for Anderson avenue. The assessments were ordered collected.

Stop Itching Torture

FOCUS ON GROUNDS, SAFETY ISSUES

The enlarged Chase school resulted in an increase in students – along with an increase in activity around the intersection of Meriden and Woodtick Roads – during the 1920s and 1930s.

Safety concerns grew in those times, as a number of traffic accidents prompted city and school officials to address the issue. A stretch of sidewalks on Meriden Road was proposed and ultimately installed (as noted in the newspaper articles on these pages), although the approval process for construction was extended over years, due to both state and city roads being involved.

And while a police officer in a patrol car is needed these days to help aid school dismissal time – when lines of cars queue up along both sides of Meriden Road to pick up students – Chase students took action back then, forming a traffic

patrol in 1937 to alert drivers at the end of the school day (see next page).

Source: Waterbury Evening Democrat

Newspaper articles from 1932 and 1935 focus on the traffic issues around H.S. Chase School.

SIDEWALK ALONG WESTERLY SIDE OF MERIDEN ROAD

May Soon Be Built From Henry Chase School to Frost Road

Construction of a sidewalk along the westerly side of Meriden road, from the Henry Chase school to Frost road, so as to eliminate the hazardous condition now existing for school children will be ordered shortly by the board of works, it has been learned. Mayor Frank Hayes is in favor of the sidewalk and will, it is understood, approve the board of works action in time to have the work carried out at about the same time that the state erects the new bridge over Mad river near the corner of Woodland avenue and Meriden road.

Scene of Accidents

The stretch of highway along Meriden road in question has been the scene of serious motor accidents and several fatalities to pedestrians. The narrow bridge

Chase School Organizes Boy Patrol In Traffic

ATTENTION! SCHOOL BEING DISMISSED

YOUNGSTERS IN ANTI-ACCIDENT CAMPAIGN

SPOTLIGHTING

Brass City News

Out Like a Lion!

March has insisted on going out like a lion this year. As a result streets of the city were covered this morning with a dangerous coating of ice and snow which caused several minor accidents, reduced motor traffic to a mini-

In the Swim

Starting Monday evening and continuing for a twelve week span, the spring term of the Red Cross swimming classes for working girls and married women will get underway at the Crosby pool, it was announced today. The spring

---

Youngsters With Signs Given Warning to Passing Autoists

In an effort to avoid the sorrow brought about, in most cases, by carelessness and to offset the possibility of unforseen accidents the 7th and 8th grade pupils at Henry S. Chase school, directed by Miss Grace C. Luddy, have formed the Chase School Boy Patrol.

Each day, at the close of school, members of this patrol stand on the curb near the building and display signs like the one seen above which warn the passing motorist that school is being dismissed. On the other hand the pupils cooperate with the car driver by refraining from dashing out into the street.

Arm of Patrol

An idea of the aims of the patrol may be gathered from some of the following excerpts taken from the charter:

Members shall serve for at least ten weeks because experience means efficiency unless necessity warrants a change. Members may be re-elected.

Duties shall consist of the following actions:

Attendance at "Safety Council Meetings." Standing at posts assigned on side walks, at exits, etc., to keep children on sidewalks at all times especially at dismissals.

Display signs ((Attention! School Being Dismissed) at three points of building to warn motorists of dismissal. Encouraging children to use crosswalks and to obey traffic officers.

State Highway Head Confers Here To-day; May Build Sidewalk

Wider and More Modern Project Planned to Eliminate Hazards to Motorists—City May Pay for Sidewalk From Chase School to Frost Road

Meriden road's bridge, famous for automobile deaths and accidents, is to be torn down and a new structure set up in its place, wider and more modern in structure it was learned to-day. At 2 o'clock this afternoon a representative of the state highway department was in conference with city officials in the office of Mayor Frank Hayes in an effort to bring about a change in the present situation. It was also learned that the conference will result in the construction of a sidewalk, on the west side of Meriden road, from Chase school to Frost road.

State To Build It

The State of Connecticut will construct the new bridge and carry out the work of tearing down the present structure. Many auto accidents, resulting in fatal or serious injuries to persons involved, have been noted during many years past.

The bridge in question is just south of the old "Green Line" car barns and it crosses the Mad River. The state officials are seeking the co-operation of the city in widening the bridge, which is now very narrow. Whether the entire expense will be borne by the state or partially borne by the city will be known after this afternoon's meeting in the mayor's office.

Sidewalk Good News

The fact that the plans call for the construction of a sidewalk on the west side of the highway, from Chase school to Frost road, is considered something of importance. During the last session of the legislature, Senator Joseph H. Lawlor of the board of works succeeded in having a bill passed providing for a commission to study the need of sidewalks for pedestrians along highways. The committee reported favorably but there was no way in which to force the state highway department to carry out the plan. Lack of funds was the excuse offered.

Since then sidewalks have been urged for the Milford turnpike, where many pedestrians have met death upon being struck by motor vehicles. In other parts of the state the cry for protection for pedestrians on state highways is being heard.

The city, it is believed, will bear the expense of building the sidewalk from Chase school to the Frost road if the city tears down and rebuilds the bridge in question.

Eliminate Hazards

The bridge is very narrow and does not meet the measurement of the road, itself. This narrowness was necessary because of the adjacent "Green Line" tracks. Now the trolleys are not running, due to the use of buses, and the widening of the bridge is possible, hence the immediate steps on the part of the state and city to eliminate the present hazard to motorists.

OBITUARY

PISANO—Luigi Pisano, age 61 years, died early this morning at the Waterbury hospital after a brief illness. Mr Pisano came to this country from Italy 46 years ago and for the first fourteen years made his home in Pennsylvania. For the past 32 years he has resided in this city where he acquired a wide acquaintance of friends. He was employed by the Chase Metal works up to five years ago when he retired.

Mr Pisano is survived by his wife, Angelina; two sons, Charles Bristol and Anthony of this city; eight daughters, Mrs Nicholas Decola, Mrs Gaetano Tiso, Mrs Aniello Giuditta, Mrs Anthony Russo, Mrs Joseph Colacci, Mrs Anthony Filippelli, Mrs Michael Marino and Mrs Joseph Folletta; 13 grandchildren, all of this city, and one brother, Michael in America.

The funeral will be held from the home, 1275 North Main street on Thursday morning at 8 o'clock to St Lucy's church where a solemn mass of requiem will be celebrated at 9 o'clock. Burial will be in Calvary cemetery.

RIVARD—Eben A. Rivard has

Source: Waterbury Evening Democrat

Articles from 1934 (at right) and 1937 describe initiatives to address traffic safety issues outside H.S. Chase elementary school.

PARKLET STAYS; NEARBY SCHOOL IS SCRAPPED

Research into Chase School's history uncovered a couple of interesting developments in the 1930s that would have altered the future development of the school.

But in the end, neither initiative came to fruition.

An effort to remove the triangular patch of grass near the front of the school had begun in 1931, as some local entities wanted to capitalize on the development in the neighborhood after the 1922-23 school expansion.

The tiny "parklet" became a major issue that year, sparking "one of the bitterest fights in the history of Waterbury's zoning law," according to a recap of a public hearing by the Waterbury Democrat.

Residents of the Mill Plain neighborhood were seemingly divided on the question of removing the parklet.

"Some want it left where it is on the grounds that it serves as an 'aisle of safety.' Others claim that it is a menace to motorists and also a dangerous spot for persons to stand while waiting for the trolley cars," noted a June 3, 1931 article in the Waterbury Democrat.

In addition, removal of the grassy patch was required for construction of a proposed gas station on the corner of Southmayd and Meriden roads.

A series of hearings were held on the proposal, with Rev. Joseph Todd of nearby Mill Plain Union Church – who was opposed to the development – involved in a heated exchange with an attorney representing the project at one session.

The city's board of works ultimately decided to retain the parklet and deny the gas station application.

And thus, 90 years later, the small triangle of grass remains near Chase School,

FAIRLAWN GRAMMAR SCHOOL MUDDLE WAS SETTLED YESTERDAY

There Will Be New Nine-Room Building at Corner of Woodland and Homestead Avenues — Plans Will Be Drawn By City Engineering Department

WHOLE MATTER ABLY DISCUSSED

Fairlawn will have a new school, to be constructed at the corner of Woodland and Homestead avenues; and the plans for this nine room grammar school unit building will be drawn by the engineering department of the city which will also supervise its construction. This, in a nutshell, constitutes the action taken at the board of education meeting yesterday at which Mayor Frank Hayes presided and brought immediate action and some semblance of order out of a prolonged fight which has lasted for some weeks.

The first business to be transacted was relative to the report of the "committee of the whole." After much discussion in connection with the matter of proper form of the recommendations and the physical make-up of the report, the members proceeded to vote on the suggestions.

That the clerk be empowered to advertise for bids for the sale of the buildings on the Fairlawn site, the bids to be in the hands of the board not later than Monday, March 30th, g

Continue Fight To Remove Parklet

Mrs Jennie McCary Offers $5,000 Toward Work, Provided Her Property Is Sold

Strenuous efforts to have the parklet in front of the Henry Chase school on Meriden road removed, [...] me [...] ars, [...] of [...] who [...] re- [...] be- [...] ar- [...] ing

the undertaking. The board took no action except to place the petition in the hands of the street committee, which has been studying the matter for many, many months.

The residents in Mill Plain are divided on the question of removing the parklet. Some want it left where it is on the grounds that it serves as an "aisle of safety." Others claim that it is a menace to motorists and also a dangerous spot for persons to stand while waiting for the trolley cars.

Mrs McCary contended that the majority of the people in the immediate vicinity favor the removal of the parklet. She objected to a few governing the question. A letter was also introduced from Rev Thomas Mulcahy, who originally signed the petition opposing the removal of the parklet. He is now convinced, he stated, that the parklet is a menace and should be removed.

It is understood that Mrs McCary will be able to sell her land, which faces the parklet, providing the little triangle is removed. A gasoline station is proposed for the place. In answer to a question con-

Source of articles: Waterbury Democrat

Newspaper articles from 1931, highlighting issues related to Chase School, along with a modern-day look at the remaining 'parklet' near the school.

even with nearly a century of further development in the neighborhood. Perhaps we can all thank Rev. Todd for the verdant frontage that continues to skirt school property.

A different development that also began in 1931 nearly resulted in a new city public school being built not far from Chase School.

In March of that year, the city's Board of Education approved plans to construct a new school at the corner of Homestead and Woodland avenues.

Land for the Fairlawn Manor School was then purchased, a number of homes were cleared and bonding for water and sewer improvements secured.

But a number of issues emerged in following years, which kept the project from moving forward.

After a decade of delay, local residents demanded the city take some action with the property, and instead of a new school, the Fairlawn neighborhood got a new playground.

Who knows how H.S. Chase School's development over the last century would have been shaped if Fairlawn School – rather than Fairlawn Park – was built less than a mile away in the 1930s?

GRADUATIONS IN THE 1930S

The H. S. Chase Grammar School

Graduating Exercises Will Take Place To-night at School Hall

Ralph Creer will present the diplomas to the members of the Henry S. Chase grammar school at the graduation exercises to be held this evening in the school auditorium.

The program to be presented follows:
Song, "Daybreak" . . . . Class
Reading, "Americanism," Walter Abel (Valedictorian).
Reading, "The Spellin' Bee" . . . . Harvey Borwn
Piano solo, "La Paloma," . . . . Gertrude Foley
Reading, "Spanish Waters" . . . . Ivy Needham
"June Song" . . . . Class
Reading, "The Inventor's Wife" . . . . Mildred Pfurr
Presentation, Gustave Stafstrom (Salutatorian).
Reply to presentation, Charles De Bisschop.
Solo, "Second Minuet," William Carpenter.
Essay, "Robert Falcon Scott," Mary Hickox (Valedictorian).
Presentation of diplomas, Mr Ralph Creer.
Class song, class.

The class officers are Gustave Stafstrom, president; Mary Hickox, vice president; Ernest Rabinson, secretary, and Walter Abel, treasurer.

Members of the graduating class are Walter Abel, Ruth Aitchison, Raymond Albert, Agnes Beauchaine, Michael Bosco, Roland Boucher, Harvey Brown, Helen Butterworth, George Bunker, William Carpenter, Antonette Dadamo, Charles De Bisschop, Michael Dervis, Gordon Dimmock, Robert Dobrick, Ger-

RECEPTION FOR CHASE PUPILS

Graduating Class Guests at Eighth Annual Dinner

Some 250 persons were present at the eighth annual dinner and entertainment given by the Chase Parent-Teacher association to the members of the graduating class at Chase school in the Mill Plain church gymnasium last night. Rev. Waights J. Henry, assistant pastor of Bunker Hill church, was the principal speaker. Other speakers were Supt. of Schools Thomas J. Condon, Mrs. Florence Bonney Webster, member of the board of education; Miss Marie Macdonnell, of Crosby high school faculty; Mrs. John Mraz, president of the association. Mrs. Tennant Elwell was given a past president's pin and Mrs.

SPEAKER

REV. WAIGHTS J. HENRY

Mraz, who was master of ceremonies, was given a corsage.

The eighth grade pupils honored

Source: Waterbury Democrat

FROST ROAD GIRL IS VALEDICTORIAN

Barbara Chamberlain Heads Graduating Class At Chase School

Barbara Chamberlain, daughter of Mr and Mrs Ross Chamberlain of 859 Frost road, was declared valedictorian of the graduating class at Henry S. Chase school this morning. Principal Sadie F. Rigney names James M. Dowling, son of Mr and Mrs James M. Dowling of 80 Woodtick road, salutatorian. Barbara maintained an average of 97.9 in all her studies during the past year. James ends his term with an average of 97.35.

Other honor students are: Over 95 per cent—Barbara Matthews, Pauline Wilcox, Corinne Hickox, Genevieve Dervis; over 90—Alice Thomas, Lillian Bonaker, Mary Rizzuto and Lina Dowling, Thomas White; over 85—Bernice Bergen, Adel Boisvert, Leonard Gauht, Fred Krawchuk, Miriam Harris, Margaret Currie, Anthony Mirabillo, David Smith, Florence Lombardo; over 80—Bernice Faero, Gertrude Stepney, Robert Knickerbocker, Louis Butterworth and William Carew, Betty Boyd, William Lafevre, Mary Dolecki, Walter Krous, David Lovallo, Harry Tchakirides and Eva Aoas, and Ruth Molinek.

William Carew who is the son of Mr and Mrs Pierce Carew of 188 Academy avenue was chosen president of the class by his fellow graduates. Barbara Matthews was

---

Old newspaper articles published in the Waterbury Democrat highlight the achievements of Chase School students during the 1930s.

At left, an outline of the 1931 graduation exercises planned at the East End school.

Above, highlights of a dinner for Chase's 1936 graduates.

At right, a story on the valedictorian and honor students in the 1934 graduating class at Chase School.

1938 COMMENCEMENT

Source: Waterbury Democrat

Chase School Honor Students

JANET ELVIN   GLORIA PRESCOTT

The two girls above are first-ranking honor students in the 1938 graduating class of Henry S. Chase school. Gloria Prescott and Janet Elvin have been leaders during their grammar school careers. The graduation exercises will be held later in the month.

Thirty years after the school's graduating class consisted of just five students, the 1938 class included 53 pupils, an indication of the growth in numbers being educated at the East End school.

The photo above shows the 1938 graduates of H.S. Chase in front of nearby Mill Plain Union Church.

Gloria Prescott and Janet Elvin, shown at left, were the top-ranking students in the Chase School class of 1938.

53 TO GRADUATE AT CHASE SCHOOL

Honor Students, Members of 1938 Class Officially Announced Today

A class of 53 students will be graduated this month from Henry S. Chase school, it was announced today by Miss Sadie F. Rigney, principal.

First ranking honor pupils in the graduating calss are Gloria Prescott and Janet Elwin. Members of the class are as follows:

Margaret Ann Decker, John P. Bilotta, Margaret Thelma Book, Elmer George Bouffard, Charles E. Case, Harland Hyde Christofferson, Leslie H. Coley, Jr., Constantine Edward Como, Floretta Creer, John F. DeBisschop, Marion Ann Dinova, Walter Richard Dressel, Dorothy M. Rugan, Arele May Edmond, Norman Conrad Elsdon, Janet Elizabeth Elwin, Doris Louis Giusto, Frank Warren Granger, John J. Grosso, Stanley B .Heaton, Henrietta Marie Howis, Louis Hercules Jamele, Gertrude Ruth Larson, Marion Margaret lefevre, Arline Dorothy Lucian, Joseph R. Luttazi, Joan E. Manson, Catherine Marie Masse, Albert Walter Matthews, Raymond John Miglaro, Mildred Evelyn Miller, Mary Mirabillio, Adele Bryan Munson, Richard E. Murphy, Edyth

SPORTING ACHIEVEMENTS

Source: Waterbury Democrat

Above, the Waterbury Democrat's account of a no-hitter tossed by Chase School pitcher Stanley Heaton on June 3, 1936.

Clipping contributed by Ray Sullivan

At right, a team photo of the 1949 Chase School baseball team, which captured a divisional title in the public school league .

Athletic events have proven to be among the most popular extracurricular activities at city schools, and the competitions go back in time for more than 100 years. Waterbury schools started an "Athletic Association" in 1908, with competitions in baseball, basketball and girls volleyball the first sporting endeavors within the system.

Chase School has had its share of winning moments over the years, some of which are featured on this and the next couple of pages.

H. S. CHASE SCHOOL BASEBALL TEAM—Pete McCasland, coach of the Chase entry in the Grammar School League, will send his squad against B. W. Tinker tomorrow afternoon at Hamilton Park at 4 o'clock in a playoff game. Al Banche and Angelo Perrone have been assigned to umpire. Front row, left to right: Robert Rangoon, James Skino, Jackie McCasland, batboy; Terry Doolady, and Peter McCasland. Second row: Billy Margaritta, Ray Sullivan, Tom Zastko, Capt. Peter Paznokas, Bernie Chieffo, Ernest Tarantina. Third row: Ray Nelson, Roy Rowe, Andrew Guiste, Carmen Caruso, Henry Oulette, and Peter McCasland, coach.—Birch Photo.

Contributed photos, clippings

Above, the gymnasium at Chase, shown as the school addition in 1951-52 was nearing completion. (Note the narrower foul lane/key, which was standard at that time.)

At right, the box score from a Chase basketball team's victory over Wilson on Dec. 20, 1944.

At left, Chase's championship cheerleading team from the late 1960s.

THIS JUBILANT group of young ladies "brought home the bacon" for H. S. Chase School Sunday afternoon by capturing the public school championship in the Park Department's third annual Girls' Cheerleading Festival at Hamilton Park field. They replace Kingsbury which had ruled the roost for the past two years. Wendell Cross finished second; Bunker Hill third. More than 160 persons witnessed the colorful event which included a parade, raising of Old Glory, and music by the Fulton American Band. Members of the championship squad shown above are: Front row, left to right—Barbara Boccia, Elizabeth Cocchiola, Eleanor Kakeky, Jane Wierbonics, Linda Walsh, and Donna Santos. Standing, left to right—Charlin Hublad, Connie Langin, Claudia LaValle, Jean Christiano, and Sandra Oliver.—Cristin Photo

Walsh And Chase Hoop Winners

Walsh and Chase were national division Public School basketball winners of games played yesterday, Walsh defeating Webster 15 to 8; while Chase was an 18 to 6 winner over Woodrow Wilson. Greatorex, scoring 11 points was high for Chase. Scores:

WALSH

	B	F	P
Patella, lf	1	0	2
Capobianco	0	0	0
Goodson, rf	2	0	4
Falph, c	0	0	0
Petriet, lg	2	0	4
Tarullo, rg	2	1	5
Jacobino	0	0	0
Totals	7	1	15

WEBSTER

	B	F	P
Manetti, rg	0	0	0
Hein, lg	0	0	0
Vertuli, c	1	0	2
George, rf	0	2	2
Martone, lf	1	2	4
Totals	2	4	8

Score at half time: Walsh 12, Webster 2. Referee: Monti.

CHASE

	B	F	P
Pollard, lf	1	0	2
Delilla	0	1	1
Delilla, rf	0	0	0
Anton	0	0	0
Lewis, c	0	0	0
P. Capozzi, lg	1	2	4
K. Greatorex, rg	3	5	11
Totals	5	8	18

WILSON

	B	F	P
Pannone, rg	1	0	2
Kalinowski, lg	1	2	4
O'Donnell, c	0	0	0
Laurenzi, rf	0	0	0
Massimo	0	0	0
Mazillo, rf	0	0	0
Totals	2	2	6

Score at half time: Chase 9, Wilson 4. Referee: Barone.

Contributed photos

Grammar League

Prin. Sadie F. Rigney's H. S. Chase School nine, thanks to a brilliant joint no-hit, no-run pitching performance by "Tex" Veillette and "Spud" DiMaria, blanked Hopeville, 3-0, at Hamilton Park yesterday afternoon to capture the championship of the Eastern section of the American Division of the Public Baseball League.

By virtue of the triumph the Mill Plainers earned the right to meet B. W. Tinker in the play-off for the Public School title at Hamilton Park No. 1

The winner will face St. Mary's Parochial titlists for the city championship later in the week.

In other Public School games yesterday, Hendricken trounced Maloney, 12-3, and National Division clashes saw Driggs conquer Slocum, 7-3, while Duggan was whitewashing Merriman 10-0, behind the one-hit pitching of Junior Zaza, who was ably abetted by some fine stickwork by Chick Clary who garnered three hits including a home run with one mate aboard.

Likely drove in two of Chase's runs with a triple and a single. Scores by innings:

H. S. Chase	030 000	3 6 1
Hopeville	000 000	0 0 0

Veillette, DiMaria (5) and Likely; O'Keefe and Gormar. Umpire—Ventresca.

Hendricken	220 350	12 3 2
Maloney	110 010	3 6 6

Rhinehart and Daniels; Dodiiena and Reynolds. Umpire Sullivan.

Driggs	013 21	7 6 3
Slocum	102 00	3 4 3

Kurtz and Roberts; Duffy and Tiso. Umpire—Banche.

Duggan	532 00	10 6 0
Merriman	000 00	0 1 0

Zaza and Lestage; Cortese, Rodriguez and Sarra. Umpire—McCowen.

Above, the 1973-74 Chase School basketball team, which won the American Division championship of Waterbury's Grammar School league. Pictured from left, first row: Dave Kirk, Vin DeVico, Mike Hoban, Walter Spencer, John Cannata and John Taplin. Second row: Coach Cass Renkun, Tony Santoro, Gary Chiarella, Rick Way, Mark Wawer, Lou Martelli and coach Charles Corden.

Top left: Pete Anton wearing his school uniform. Pete would go on to earn All-City and All-NVL honors while at Crosby High, and was recipient of the city's Jack Cullinan Award for sportmanship during his senior season in 1976.

Bottom left, the Chase School cheerleading team from 1972. Members included Judy Rutka, Cathy Leogrande, Pam Christiano, Toni Gentile, Cindy Willette, Gail Giacin, Lori Iannacone and Victori Bonacassio.

At right, a recap of the game that gave the 1949 Chase team (pictured on previous page) its divisional title.

Chase, Sprague Hoop Winners

Chase grammar school basketball team was a 22 to 19 winner of a close and interesting game with Barnard played yesterday at Barnard. The game was played for the Infantile Paralysis fund and the teams were never more than a few points apart. McWilliams, with 11 points and White with six scored well for the winners; Jamele and Palladino getting 11 for Barnard.

East End Clubs Sponsor Party

The Chase-Parent Teachers' association and the East End Community club will sponsor a card party on March 10. The proceeds of the affair, which will be held at the new gymnasium of the Anderson school, will be donated to the Chase school basketball team.

Individual table prizes and door prizes will be presented, and refreshments served.

Among the members of the Parent-Teachers' association, who will serve on the arrangements committee are: Mrs. Bertel Stigberg, Mrs. Reginald K. Haynes, Mrs. William Gaunt, Mrs. Joseph LaVallee, Mrs. Earl Fenn, Mrs. Harry VanHorsten, Mrs. Raymond Fowler, Mrs. Richard Smith, Mrs. Robert Likley, Mrs. Ernest Bock, Mrs. Albert Spagnola, Mrs. A. Verrastro, Mrs. John Albert,

Source: Waterbury Democrat

Newspaper clippings above highlight a Chase School basketball victory during the team's 1943-44 season (at top), and an announcement for a fundraising event for the school basketball team in 1942.

1951 GRADUATION

Contributed by Ray Sullivan

Members of the 1951 graduating class at H.S. Chase elementary school gather for a photo, one that remains in Ray Sullivan's collection of memorabilia 70 years later. Ray (pictured in the third row, fourth from right) grew up just across the street from Chase School on the corner of Mansfield Avenue, in what he believes is the second oldest house in the Mill Plain section. He went on to Crosby High, Brown University and then earned a medical degree from Georgetown University. After a residency in surgery at Waterbury Hospital, Ray entered the U.S. Air Force as a Major and served as Chief of Surgical Services at Shaw AFB Regional Hospital in South Carolina. Returning home, Ray served for 30 years in General and Oncology Surgery with Surgical Associates of Waterbury (ending his time there as Chief of Staff). Set to retire soon, he has been a Director of Public Health in Brookfield for the past 13 years.

1951-52 REMODELING AND ADDITION

Contributed / H.S. Chase School

Above, workers put the finishing touches on a new classroom at Chase School, prior to the opening of the 1951-52 school year.

Below, a view of the front of the older Mill Plain School, which was taken down during the renovation in 1951.

"Things were never like this when I went to school.' That was the sentiment of more than 1,500 people who visited the remodeled and enlarged and generally transformed Chase School at the open house last night," began an article in the Waterbury Republican newspaper on March 27, 1952.

Nearly 50 years after a school was built on the site and some 30 years after an enlargement, H.S. Chase elementary school underwent another renovation, which cost about $750,000 and included 12 new classrooms, two special rooms for home economics and industrial arts, two multiple purpose rooms and a combination gymnasium-auditorium.

Work on the addition, which was

Photos contributed by H.S. Chase School

Steel framework being erected for the addition to H.S. Chase School in 1951.

28

'The atmosphere will be elevated and stimulating ...'

– Dr. John G. Gilmartin, superintendent of Waterbury schools, speaking about the renovated H.S. Chase school in 1952

designed by architect Francis L. S. Mayers, was begun by the Waterbury Construction Co. in February 1951. Double sessions at the school were required for much of the 1951-52 school year to accommodate the renovation work, which was completed in March 1952.

The renovation marked the largest project within the city school system in more than two decades, when B.W. Tinker School was enlarged in 1931. The only major school construction in the previous 20 years was the addition of a gymnasium at Anderson School in 1941; the last completely-new school constructed in the city before Chase's remodel was Wilson School in 1929.

With pastel-painted classrooms, linoleum covered floors and tiled corridors, the modern school was unveiled to the public on March 26, 1952. Dr. John G. Gilmartin, superintendent of Waterbury schools, and Dr. Harold Perkinson, president of the School Board, were on hand for the event.

"The atmosphere will be elevated and stimulating" for parents and children, Dr. Gilmartin said in the newspaper article covering the remodeled school. "Everything is conducive to work," he added, anticipating that many parents would be "somewhat bewildered" at the

Enlarged, Remodeled Chase School Offers Many Modern Improvements

Photos contributed by H.S. Chase School and the Gottscho-Schleisner collection at the Library of Congress

New classrooms built during the 1951-52 reconstruction featured ample cabinet and closet space (example at left).

The midde image above shows the new industrial arts room.

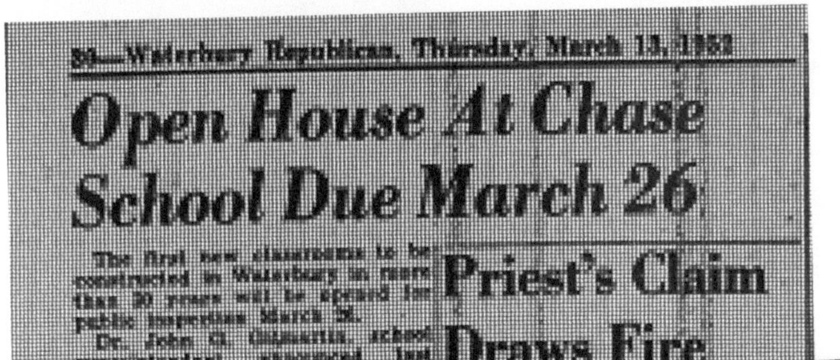

Open House At Chase School Due March 26

Priest's Claim Draws Fire

The first new classrooms to be constructed in Waterbury in more than 20 years will be opened for public inspection March 26.

Dr. John G. Gilmartin, school superintendent, announced last night that an open house will be

improvements in the school facilities from the time they attended classes.

Perkinson expressed his appreciation and thanks to Mayor Raymond. E. Snyder, the Boards of Finance and Aldermen and Budget Director Arnold E. Furlong "for their assistance and cooperation in making possible this fine addition and extensive alterations at Chase School."

He also thanked Miss Sadie F. Rigney, principal at Chase, and the school faculty, for their cooperation during construction. Miss Rigney greeted the guests in the

main lobby of the school at the event, while members of the faculty described the various features of the rooms to the visitors.

The new classrooms featured moveable furniture, fluorescent lights, and each was equipped with a sink and ample closet and cabinet space. Recessed storage lockers were installed in the new hallways.

A highlight for open house visitors was the new auditorium-gymnasium, which featured an acoustical ceiling and a stage equipped with colored lights and fireproof curtains. Folding bleachers on

Photos contributed by the Gottscho-Schleisner collection at the Library of Congress

A new modern entrance on the Woodtick Road side (shown at left) was among the additons to Chase School in 1951-52.

One of the new classrooms constructed that school year is shown above.

either side could seat 400 people, while 600 folding chairs (to set up for events) were stored under the stage.

Shower rooms for both boys and girls were added, adjoining the gymnasium, which also features its own entrance from the school yard.

The modernized school also included a new industrial arts room with modern machines and a separate lumber room, as well as a large home economics room – complete with five electric sewing machines and three kitchen units with range, sink and cabinets.

A new suite was constructed for the school nurse in the basement of the school, which featured a waiting room, an exam room, a rest room, and a large office.

Photos contributed by H.S. Chase School and the Gottscho-Schleisner collection at the Library of Congress

Dignitaries on hand for the unveiling of the remodeled H.S. Chase School included, from left, Francis L. S. Mayers, architect for the project; Dr. Harold Perkinson, president of the Board of Education; Miss Sadie F. Rigney, school principal, Dr. John G. Gilmartin, superintendent of Waterbury Schools; and William Daddona, president of Waterbury Construction Co.

Photos at right show new areas of the school, including the combination gymnasium-auditorium and a home economics room that featured multiple kitchen units and an area for sewing machines.

CHASE'S PARENT-TEACHER ASSOCIATION

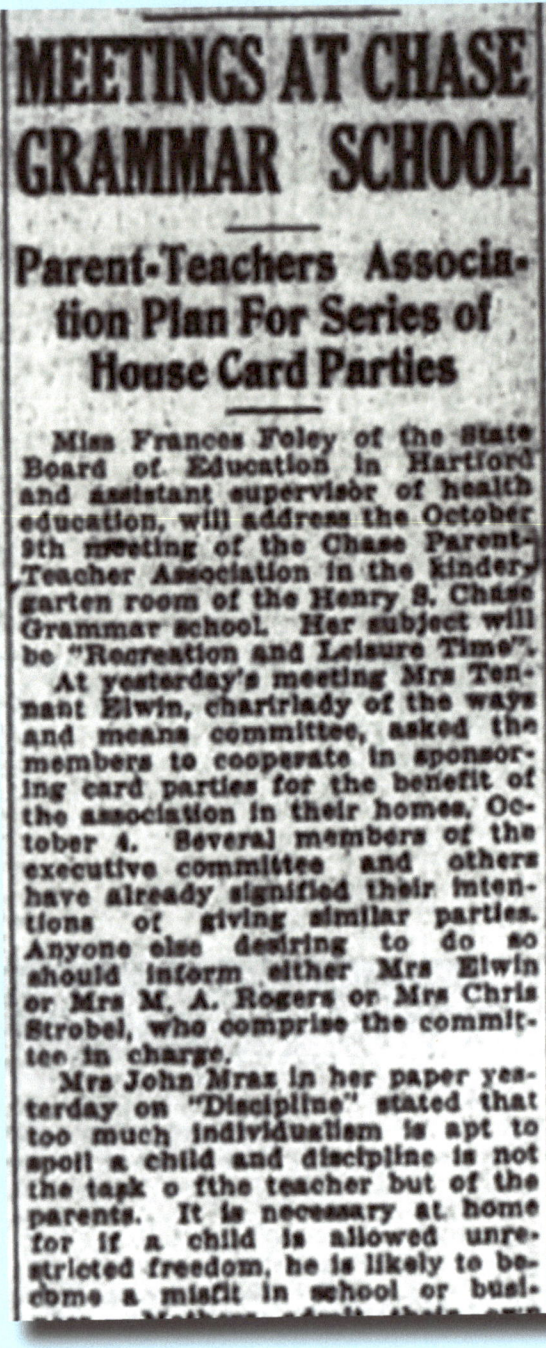

MEETINGS AT CHASE GRAMMAR SCHOOL

Parent-Teachers Association Plan For Series of House Card Parties

Miss Frances Foley of the State Board of Education in Hartford and assistant supervisor of health education, will address the October 9th meeting of the Chase Parent-Teacher Association in the kindergarten room of the Henry S. Chase Grammar school. Her subject will be "Recreation and Leisure Time".

At yesterday's meeting Mrs Tennant Elwin, chairlady of the ways and means committee, asked the members to cooperate in sponsoring card parties for the benefit of the association in their homes, October 4. Several members of the executive committee and others have already signified their intentions of giving similar parties. Anyone else desiring to do so should inform either Mrs Elwin or Mrs M. A. Rogers or Mrs Chris Strobel, who comprise the committee in charge.

Mrs John Mraz in her paper yesterday on "Discipline" stated that too much individualism is apt to spoil a child and discipline is not the task o fthe teacher but of the parents. It is necessary at home for if a child is allowed unrestricted freedom, he is likely to become a misfit in school or busi-

Throughout its history, H.S. Chase School has had a strong Parent-Teacher Association, which has helped to strengthen the partnership between families and the school over the years. Consisting of dedicated volunteers, the group has aimed to address issues that are important to parents and public school administrators, implement school improvement programs and offer entertaining extracurricular activities to enhance the Chase community.

Programs and initiatives throughout the decades highlighted on these pages include informational sessions at regular meetings, fundraising events such as card parties and recipe booklets, and plenty of activities to help nurture Chase students.

CARD PARTY

SPONSORED BY CHASE P. T. A.

for

WATERBURY HIGHER EDUCATION, INC.

CHASE SCHOOL GYMNASIUM

Friday, February 26, 1954 - 8 o'clock

Admission 62 Cents - Tax 13 Cents - Total 75 Cents

Source: Waterbury Democrat

A September 1933 meeting of the Chase School Parent-Teacher Association is detailed in the newspaper article at left. Attendees learned that a member of the state Board of Education was tapped to speak to the group about 'Recreation and Leisure Time,' that members were needed to assist with upcoming card parties, and the importance of discipline in the home to keep children from becoming 'a misfit in school.'

The article at right covers a 1936 gathering of the Chase PTA, which featured a talk on fashion trends as well as the awarding of a trophy to the group in recognition of its 100 percent rate of subscription to the state magazine.

FASHION LECTURE GIVEN CHASE P.T.A.

A talk on the fall trend in fashions was given last night by Mrs. Maria Shaw at a meeting of the Chase Parent-Teacher Association at the Henry Chase school. The speaker showed a number of samples and also discussed the remodeling of clothing. A trophy was given the group by Mrs. Jessie Bush, State magazine chairman of the Connecticut Parent-Teacher Association. The trophy was in recognition of the 100 per cent subscription of the Chase group to the state magazine.

Because the Chase school will be closed tomorrow in observance of Armistice Day the dramatic class of the association, sponsored by the WPA, will not hold the session at the school, but at the home of Mrs. Mary A. Charpentier on Meriden road.

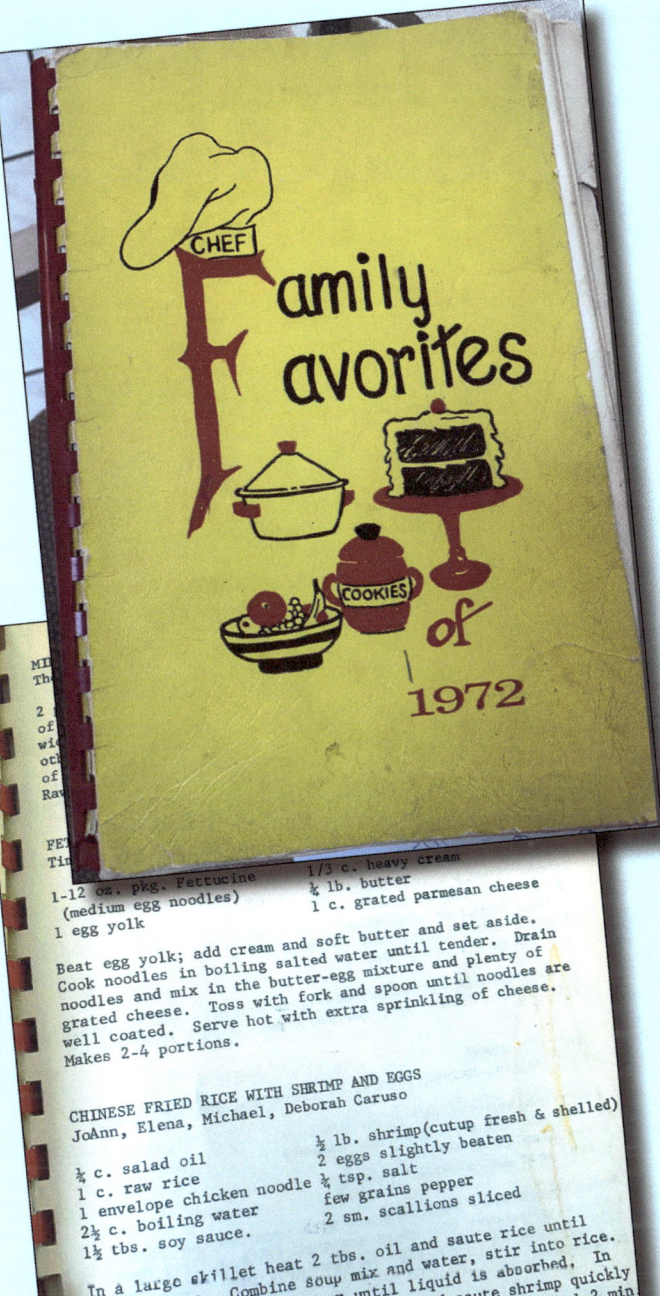

FAMILY

FAVORITE RECIPES

OF THE

H.S. CHASE SCHOOL CHILDREN

Compiled and edited

by the

H.S. Chase Parent-Teachers Association

1972 Edition

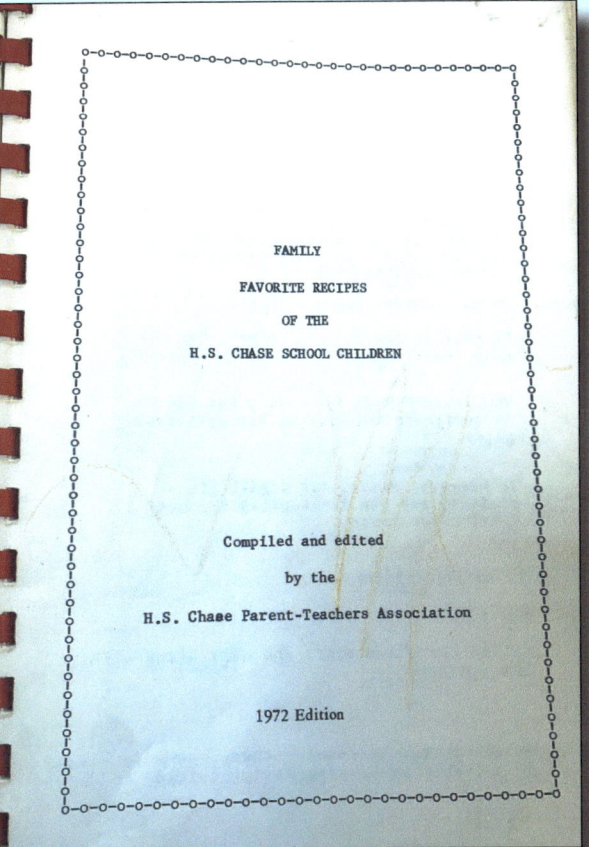

Booklet photos contributed by Michael Griffin

A compilation of recipes submitted by Chase students on behalf of their families proved to be a popular undertaking by the Parent-Teacher association in 1972. A number of former students still retain their recipe book, 50 years after its printing.

Source: Waterbury Democrat

A newspaper article (at right) recaps a Chase School PTA meeting in 1933, when new association officers were elected and when the group discussed the collection and distribution of clothes for needy children, along with the association's efforts to voice opposition to proposed reduction in funding for art instruction in schools.

H. S. CHASE SCHOOL PARENT-TEACHERS

Elected Officers at Annual Meeting Held in Mill Plain Church

INTERESTING PROGRAM

Mrs Quirino Santoro was named president of the Henry S. Chase School Parent-Teacher Association at the annual meeting last evening in the Mill Plain church rooms, succeeding Mrs C. Tennant Elwin who declined reelection. Mrs John Mraz was chosen vice-president. Mrs Ernest Kronvall, secretary, Mrs Dena Charpentier treasurer, and Mrs James Dowling, historian.

Mrs Eunice M. Clark, chairman of the student aid committee, complimented Miss Sadie F. Rigney, school principal, for her untiring efforts in distributing clothes among needy children of the institution. She also lauded the donors of the garments for putting them in condition before distribution. Funds for this work were secured through cookie and pussywillow sales and through contributions of association members.

The same speaker, reporting for the art committee, asserted that protests had been forwarded to Senators William Hackett and Harvey L. Thompson at Hartford condemning the proposed reduction in expenditures which would curtail or eliminate entirely art instructions in the schools.

33

GRAPHS GRADUATIONS IN THE 1950S/60S

Contributed photos

H.S. Chase graduates in 1959, with class list at left.

The Class of 1963, which included Louis D'Abramo, who would go on to earn a Ph.D. at Yale, become world renowned in the aquaculture field, and – like Henry Sabin Chase – be named to Silas Bronson Library's Waterbury Hall of Fame.

Members of the Chase class of 1966, which included four sets of twin boys – Dom and Henry Aurigemma, Charles and Carm Famiglietti, Ray and Rich Hawley, and Larry and Lou Zarella.

CLASS OF 1969

Thomas Adkins
Douglas Anton
Laurine Baker
John Barstis
Darlene Basil
Frederick Bernier
Donald Boisvert
Dwight Branco
Marcia Brandt
Debra Brown
Gary Brown
Claudia Calabrese
Donna Capristo
David Carroll
Edward Christiano
James Christiano
Deborah Christolini
Cheryl Codianne
Marcia Crispino
Paul Cullen
Steven Daddona
Victoria Daddona
William Demiris
Donna DiCarlo
Joseph Donahue
Alice DosSantos
Rita DosSantos
Roseann DosSantos
Dennis Elkovich
David Elwell
David Emmons
Patricia Ermini
Pasquale Flammia
Anthony Forino
Kathleen Forino
Cindy Fusco
Lawrence Fusco
Patricia Generali
Joseph Gentile
Odette George
Lorraine Giacin
Catherine Guerrera
Moira Gryniuk
Corinne Haddad
Norinne Haddad
Martin Hogrefe
Thomas Hogrefe

Joyce Hogue
Steven Honyotski
John Hunt
Vincent Iannaccone
Stephen Jager
Frederic Jarjura
James Kenworthy
Paul Lanouette
Jacqueline LaVallee
Sharon Lavigne
Debra Lebel
Carl Makarewich
Lillian Martinez
Ralph Mastracchio
Thomas Maxwell
Andrew Mazzeo
Stephen Morin
Maureen O'Hearn
Ernest Ouellette
Sharon Ouellette
Kenneth Pestone
Richard Rinaldi
Anthony Rousseau
Wendy Ruegg
Donna Santaguida
Robert Santopietro
Gloria Santoro
Robert Scannell
Gordon Strachan
James Schiavo
Paul Schiavo
Nancy Sciascia
Kim Seatts
Alton Taylor
Keith Taylor
John Testa
Gary Veneziano
William Ververis
Maureen Walsh
Michael Wawer
Nancy White
Susan Williams
Susan Yarrington
Robin Yovina
Stanley Zaksewicz
Susan Zembruski

GRADUATION
PROGRAM

—o—

Processional .... Pomp and Circumstance

Invocation .... The Lord is My Shepherd .... Class

Welcome .... Robin Yovina

Introduction to Program .... Kenneth Pestone

"My Fair Lady"

(Chase School Version)

Presentation of Class Gift .... Larry Fusco

Acceptance .... Angela Marie Zanett

Introduction of Speaker .... Gloria Santoro

Presentation of Diplomas .... Mr. Angelo Santoro

Acknowledgment of Awards

Poems — Friendship .... Victoria Daddona

Dedicated to —
Mrs. Louise Chieffo
Miss Margaret Fitzpatrick
Mrs. Grace Hansen

Farewell .... Gary Brown

H. S. CHASE SCHOOL

Graduation Exercises

WATERBURY, CONNECTICUT

Class of 1969

C

TUESDAY
JUNE TWENTY-FOURTH
NINETEEN HUNDRED SIXTY-NINE

Photo, items contributed by Debra Parry

A large graduating class gathers for the 1969 ceremony, above, with program pages below.

H.S. CHASE GRADUATION DAY IN 1968

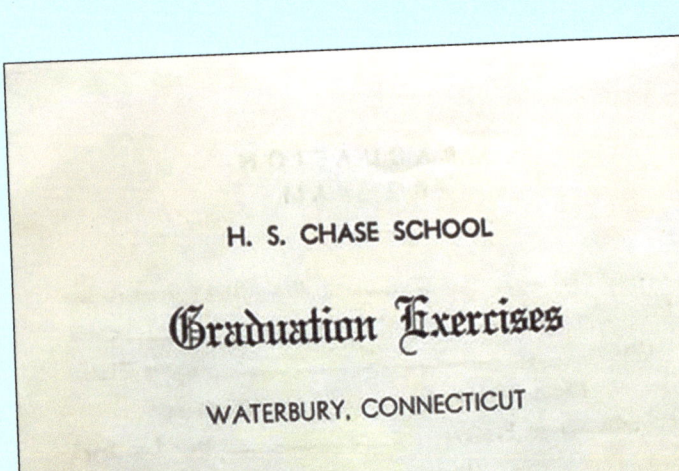

H. S. CHASE SCHOOL

Graduation Exercises

WATERBURY, CONNECTICUT

Class of 1968

THURSDAY
JUNE TWENTIETH
NINETEEN HUNDRED SIXTY-EIGHT

*Photo and items contributed
by Arthur and Vera Jarjura*

CHASE SCHOOL

Graduation Exercises

THURSDAY MORNING, JUNE TWENTIETH

NINETEEN HUNDRED SIXTY-EIGHT

AT ELEVEN O'CLOCK

June 20, 1968

The City of Waterbury

awards this

Diploma

to certify that

ARTHUR JOSEPH JARJURA

has completed the prescribed course of study in

H. S. Chase Grammar School

Waterbury, Connecticut   June 21

Marie J. Kunkel
Principal

George Harla...
Mayor and Chair...
Board ...

Michael F. Wallace
Superintendent of Schools

Salvatore G. ...
President, Board ...

Items contributed by Arthur and Vera Jarjura

GRADUATION PROGRAM

—o—

Processional	Pomp and Circumstance
Invocation	The Lord Is My Sheperd ———— Class
Welcome	Robin Finlay
Piano Selection	Jean Fischang
Introduction to Program	Roy Lockhart

Pier Gynt - Grieg

String Trio	Elaine Sciascia / Lynn Ruggiero / Robin Finlay
Accompanist	Joanne Corpaci

D. A. R. Eliza Gorman Essay Contest

First Prize Winner	Elaine Sciascia
Presentation of Class Gift	Ronnie Tirendi
Acceptance	Robin Yovina
Farewell	Patricia Stere
Piano Selection	Joanne Corpaci
Introduction to Speaker	Denise Diogostine
Presentation of Diplomas	Miss Emma Terrill

Awards

Tribute to Our Fighting Men	William LaVallee

The American Creed —— Timothy Colavecchio, Thomas Mazurek, Peter Piperas, Richard Stanco, John Strachan, Luquency Taylor } Honor Boys

Prayer for Peace	Class
Processional	The Challenge ———— Class

HONOR STUDENTS

—o—

Joanne Corpaci	Elise Pelosi
Robin Finlay	Lynn Ruggiero
Jean Fischang	Elaine Sciascia
William LaVallee	Patricia Stere
Roy Lockhart	John Strachan
Thomas Mazurek	

SCENES FROM THE NEIGHBORHOOD

"It takes a village to raise a child." So goes the proverb which suggests that an entire community of people must provide for and interact positively with children for those youngsters to grow in a safe and healthy environment.

Such communities expand beyond a child's home and school, involving lessons learned and activities experienced within a broader sphere. For many Chase students, our nurturing "village" involved shared experiences at a number of neighboring locales outside of school. Whether the purpose was for work or play, religious or Scouting services, athletic endeavors or other social gatherings – readers will surely recall the sights around Mill Plain and the East End shown on this and the next few pages.

Naugatuck Valley Mall

Contributed photos

Pictured at top left is Charlie from Charlie's Market, the convenience store that was located just across the street from Chase. Shown above is nearby Martin's drug store, in 1940.

Top left, the Mad River Grange hall, not far from Chase School (the building now houses Motion Church); bottom left, the Mad River Dam, behind Mill Plain Church and a shortcut to and from the Fairlawn neighborhood. Shown at right are some food favorites in the area: Carvel, John's Apizza, and Helen's Bakery.

At left, former Chase students are among the youngsters pictured at Perillo's Lanes, a short walk from H.S. Chase School. Photos on the right show winter and summer scenes at Hamilton Park, another spot frequented by many when school was not in session.

A pair of East End churches located not far from Chase are pictured at left: Mill Plain Union Church (top) and Sts. Peter and Paul Church. Top right shows the Green Line trolley passing the waiting station near Chase School on Meriden Road. The waiting station remains in place (shown at bottom fight corner).

CLASS PHOTOS FROM THE 1970S

THE FINAL 8TH-GRADE CLASS AT CHASE

CLASS OF 1974

Annes, Michael
Anton, Craig
Arciero, Mark
Assif, Richard
Baker, Paul
Bandeira, Kathleen
Barnett, Ruth Ann
Barringer, Brian
Becker, Philip
Belanger, Steven
Bennett, James
Bochicchio, Joseph
Boniecki, Robert
Brown, Kevin
Brown, Sandra
Burgio, Frank
Caffrey, Patrick
Caffrey, Patricia
Caruso, Elena
Christiano, Mary Ann
Cialfi, Denise
Citriniti, Elaine
Ciullo, Mark
Colavecchio, Ann
Commendatore, Christopher
Cook, Cindy
Cronin, William
Cullen, John
Dadamo, Michael
Dellofrano, Denise
Demiris, Gregory
DeVico, Vincent
Donovan, Ann Marie
Doyle, Terence
Einik, Lori
Elkovich, Donna
Emmons, Roger
Emmons, Russell
Farina, Melissa
Favale, Elaine
Flammia, Debbie
Fusco, Domenick
Gaetano, John
Galvin, Nancy
Gardiner, Candee
George, Juanita
George, Patricia
Hawley, Donna
Hicks, Addie
Hinman, Philip
Hoban, Michael
Hogrefe, Theresa
Iannaccone, Janice
Ianniello, Gina

Izzo, Steven
Johnson, Sara
Karter, David
Keane, Gerald
Kowtko, Mark
Kozlosky, Cheryl
Kulesza, Stephen
LaBonte, Brenda
Lanza, Gale
LaVallee, Eugene
LaVallee, Susan
Lebel, Lisa
Loomis, Mark
Lucian, Clifford
Mantino, Gina
Marangio, Cynthia
Mastracchio, Richard
Maxwell, Susan
McDermott, Kathleen
McGrath, Ellen
Mitchell, Scott
Morin, Holly
Morrissey, Susan
Murphy, Kevin
Norris, Maureen
O'Sullivan, Debra
Petitti, David
Perillo, Matthew
Phelan, John
Richardelli, Crista
Romaniello, Catherine
Rutka, Carolyn
SanAngelo, Michael
St. Pierre, Claude
Santa Barbara, Concetta
Santarsiero, Paula
Santoro, Judith
Schlander, Robert
Sheehan, Christine
Spencer, Kevin
Spencer, Walter
Stokes, Kathy
Sundell, Kathleen
Taplin, Johnnie
Timm, Ann Marie
Trocchi, Luciana
Uriano, Joan
Valonis, Maxine
Veneziano, Barbara
Violante, Judith
Wawer, Mark
Way, Patrick
Wihbey, Francis
Williams, Richard

GRADUATION PROGRAM

PROCESSIONAL ———— Pomp and Circumstance ————— Class
INVOCATION ———— The Lord Is My Shepherd ———— Class
WELCOME ————————————— Catherine Romaniello
INTRODUCTION TO PROGRAM ——————— Mark Wawer

THE HISTORY and SONGS of OUR COUNTRY
FROM 1900 - 1974

1920 - 1930	Maureen Norris
1930 - 1940	Mark Arciero
1940 - 1950	Mark Ciullo
1950 - 1960	Richard Assif
1960 - 1970	Donna Hawley
1970 - 1974	Elena Caruso

PRESENTATION OF CLASS GIFT —————— Ann Colavecchio
Acceptance - Matthew Cullen

REMARKS ————————————— Joseph Skerritt

PRESENTATION OF DIPLOMAS:
Edward F. Ryan   Cass Renkun
Thomas L. McKinney   Carl G. Parrillo
Daniel V. Romaniello

ACKNOWLEDGEMENT OF AWARDS ———— Joseph Cavanaugh
FAREWELL ————————————— David Petitti
PRAYER FOR PEACE ————————————— Class
RECESSIONAL ———— The Entertainer ———— Class
Pianist - Scott Mitchell

HONOR STUDENTS

Mark Arciero	Cynthia Marangio
Steven Belanger	Richard Mastracchio
Patricia Caffrey	Kathleen McDermott
Elena Caruso	Scott Mitchell
Ann Colavecchio	Maureen Norris
Denise Dellorfano	Catherine Romaniello
Lori, Einik	Carolyn Rutka
Donna Hawley	Judy Santoro
Mark Loomis	Mark Wawer

Graduation photo and program contributed by Lori Anton-Ritch; class photos contributed by H.S. Chase School

With the Waterbury school system moving away from a K-8 setup and incorporating the middle-school concept into its educational framework in the mid-1970s, graduates in 1974 represented the final class to complete eighth grade at H.S. Chase School. Photos on this spread of pages show the Class on 1974 on graduation day, along with class photos of two of the eighth-grade classes that school year.

H. S. CHASE SCHOOL

Graduation Exercises

Waterbury, Connecticut

Class of 1974

C

TUESDAY

JUNE TWENTY-FIFTH

NINETEEN HUNDRED SEVENTY-FOUR

9:00 A.M.

DEVELOPMENTS IN THE 1970S

Contributed photos

Portable classrooms, installed in the early 1970s at Chase School, are pictured in a 1972 photo shown above. The lower photos is a modern-day look at Crosby High School, part of a complex that also included Wallace Middle School that opened for the 1974-75 school year.

A number of changes highlighted the decade of the 1970s at H.S. Chase School in Waterbury.

A section of portable classrooms was added to the school's landscape in the early 1970s, to accomodate some overflow in the student body.

Chase's student body would see a more dramatic change for the 1974-75 school year. An impressive new complex on Pierpont Road opened in September of that year, housing the relocated Crosby High School along with the new Wallace Middle School.

City officials had opted to restructure Waterbury's school system, moving away from a kindergarten-to-eighth grade setup for its grammar schools and incorporating the middle-school concept into its framework. The middle schools would serve students from sixth grade through eighth grade, meaning that Chase and other elementary schools would thus begin to only teach students through the fifth grade.

The decision meant that a number of Chase teachers would also move on to join the staff at Wallace, the first of three middle schools that would open in Waterbury during the 1970s.

And while that would certainly change the face of Chase School, its appearance was physically altered for a bit after a pair of minor fires, pictured on the next page, in the late 1970s.

Fire damages Chase School

By JACK GOLDBERG

A fire in Chase School Monday night caused heavy damage in a kindergarten room and filled the rest of the school with smoke.

Principal Joseph Skerritt said school will be open today with classes in the kindergarten room and two nearby second grade rooms that suffered water damage transferred to other rooms.

Fire Chief I. C. DelBuono said the fire appeared to begin in a cloakroom that was also used for supplies and was located next to the kindergarten room. It spread to the nearby kindergarten room on the east side of the building.

Deputy Chief Thomas B. Cavanaugh said the fire was mostly contained in the ceiling tiles of the kindergarten and cloak rooms.

Dr. Michael Wallace, superintendent of schools, said he wouldn't have an estimate of monetary damage until today.

DelBuono said police detectives were at the scene investigating in case it should be later determined the blaze was of suspicious origin. He said that there was no suspicion of any possible origin of the fire right now.

He said there was quite a bit of smoke damage throughout both floors of the sprawling building on Meriden and Woodtick roads. About 550 students attend the school.

The fire was discovered by a custodian who called it into the fire department at 7:41 p.m.

Walls were blackened on the first floor by smoke while the corridor where the kindergarten room is located had water on it 3 inches high. Ceiling tiles were knocked down by firemen and some windows were broken.

Firemen were sweeping up debris with shovels and tossing it out of the broken windows.

Mayor Edward D. Bergin Jr., who was at the scene, said the windows would be boarded up until repairs are made.

Middlebury and Watertown volunteer fire departments brought smoke ejectors to the scene to aid Waterbury firefighters.

Detective Lt. Ernest Deal said a photog-

case there was something to be found, he said.

No firefighters were injured although one temporarily suffered smoke inhalation. He was all right after a few minutes outside.

Ladders were thrown up around the school but only the smallest one against the first-floor window where the smoke was pouring from was used.

Engines 2, 5, 7, 10, Trucks 2 and 3 and the emergency car responded to the fire.

The school was hit by fire in October of 1977 when a propane torch was left on by a workman and ignited ceiling tiles in a second-floor classroom. Damage was minor.

Contributed / H.S. Chase School

EXTRACURRICULAR ACTIVITIES

CHASE SCHOOL PUPIL WINNER

Marjorie German Captures First Honors in WATR Spelling Contest

Registration showed an increase in yesterday's WATR spelling bee as Marjorie German of 245 Atwood avenue, a pupil in the seventh grade at Henry S. Chase school, won out over eleven other contestants. Second place went to Leonard Schiavo of Merriman and third honors to Beatrice Machin, also of Chase school.

The match was held yesterday under the supervision of Studio Manager George Duffy and pupils from five local grammar schools participated. On last Friday only five contestants entered the match, but interest seems to have been renewed, what with twelve entries for yesterday's contest. A complete list of entrants follows:

Aurora Queiroga, 27 River street, Merriman; Celeste Queiroga, 27 River street, Merriman; Helen Teach, 242 Woodtick road, Chase; Doris Charbonneau, 117 Stilson road, Chase; Olga Anastasio, 461 Homestead avenue, Chase; Marjorie German, 245 Atwood avenue, Chase; Antoinette Genoa, 47 Ayer street, Merriman; Doris Sullivan, 217 Atwood avenue, SS. Peter and Paul;

Article clip from the Waterbury Democrat; photos contributed by Maria Burns, Katie Velez and the Gottscho-Schleisner collection at the Library of Congress

This compilation of photographs and newspaper clippings focuses on a number of extracurricular activities at Chase School over the years.

The Waterbury Democrat article at left details the results of a 1936 spelling bee for grammar school students, won by Marjorie German of H.S. Chase.

Above, students practice a song for a musical performance in 1952.

At top right, Chase principal Joseph Skerritt watches as Roxanne Russell and Frances Duff show off their technique during a Jump-a-thon for the Waterbury Heart Association in 1983, when fourth- and fifth-graders from H.S. Chase raised $1,500 for the association.

At bottom right, fourth-grade teacher Joanne Byrne adjusts the rabbit ears on student Meghan Griffin before the class performs a play to mark National Library Month in April 1988.

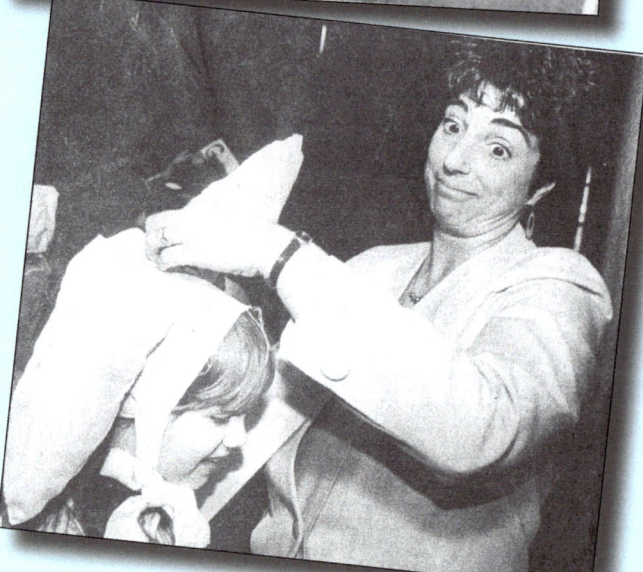

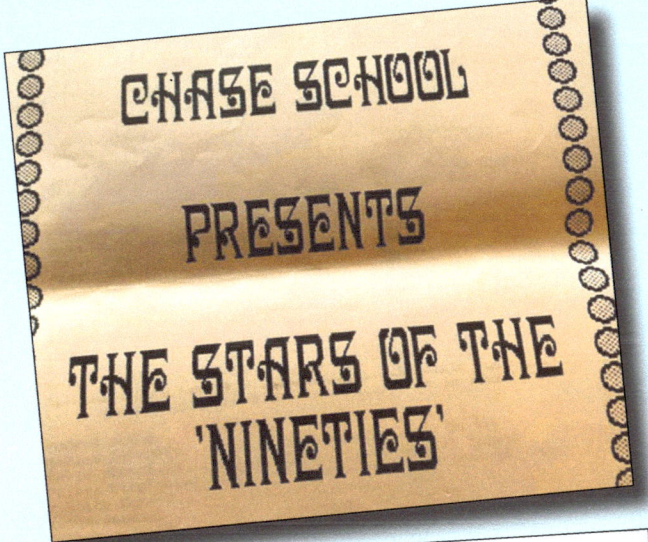

CHASE SCHOOL

PRESENTS

THE STARS OF THE 'NINETIES'

GRADES ONE AND THREE

MAR.14'74 – JUNE.14'74

HERE LIES
Mr. RAY ZOR
"He was always Dull"

"Lost in the
Battle of the
Whiskers"

*Photos/items contributed by Roxanne Russell,
Erica Tutino and H.S. Chase School*

THE STARS OF THE 'NINETIES'
FEBRUARY 2, 1990

KINDERGARTEN
Michelle Rinaldi......................Please Don't Go Girl
Daniel Englehard....................Heard It Through the Grapevine
Melissa Guisto........................This One's For the Children
Craig Piel...............................Batman
Katie Falstreau.......................Rainbow Connection

FIRST GRADE
Amber Perez...........................Bad
Jessica Anzivine.....................I Think We're Alone Now
Maritza Otano/
Jacqueline Mancuso/Jason Gugliotti......Barbie and the Rockers

SECOND GRADE
Victoria Perez........................Right Stuff
Brett Downs...........................Batdance
Pamela Laliberte....................Bust A Move
Robyn Gravel.........................Walk Like An Egyptian
William Englehard...................Old Time Rock & Roll

THIRD GRADE
Anne Marie Velez....................Blame it on the Rain
Emily Dunn............................Hangin' Tough
Marc DiDominzio...................Surfin' USA
Melissa Martino......................Girls Just Want to Have Fun
Katherine Haines.....................Right Stuff
Marcie Guisto.........................Last Night I Saw Santa Claus
Doug Donahoo........................Put Me In Coach
Tracee Beazer.........................Miss You Much
Daphne Couture/
Jean Tardy/Stacy Tardy.............My Boyfriend's Back
Besa Asani/Diana Fischer...........Right Stuff
Erin Falstreau/Leanne Dillon......Electric Youth
Katie Moser/Cristin Cook...........Lost in Your Eyes

FOURTH GRADE
Miriam Torres........................Tell Me Why
Kevin Blanchard.....................Splish Splash
Chiara Strziewski....................Cold Hearted Snake
Timothy Scheid.......................Rock On
Kevin Neuman........................Heaven
Dianna D'Ambrosio.................Straight Up
Traci DiFronzo......................Staying Together
Lishada Perry.........................Don't Make Me Over
Jason Blanchard.....................Wolly Bully
Richard Rappi........................Faith
Shane Downs..........................Stop it Girl
Ronnie Duntz.........................Beth
Robert Macary........................Great Balls of Fire
James Piel..............................Batman

CHASE SCHOOL NEWS
MAY

The City of Waterbury is an equal opportunity employer.

Parents may visit the school anytime but if a conference is requested, please call ahead for an appointment.

Highlight of Month

On Tuesday, April 28th Mr. Lloyd Bronson of the National Aeronautics and Space Administration visited Chase School. Through an interesting demonstration lecture, with the use of simple experiments and scale models of space hardware, basic scientific principles were explained. The boys and girls were updated in the area of air and space exploration. We all have an increased awareness and understanding of scientific research and technological development in the world of today.

Attendance Awards   Third Marking Period

       Grade 1 Miss Arciero   95.5
              2 Mrs. Shalagan   96.6
              3 Mrs. Shambreskis   95.5
              4 Miss Alexinski   93.3
              5 Mr. Romaniello   93.5

The second grades had the best average - 95.5.

Twenty-seven students have perfect attendance.

The Cognitive Ability Test scores for kindergarten, Grade three and grade five have been received. Parents have the opportunity to request a conference and review these scores.

Field Trips

May 7th   The fourth grade classes of Mrs. Calmar and Miss Alexinski will visit the Indian Institute in Washington, Connecticut.

May 18th   Miss Arciero, Mrs. Gwisdala and Miss Carpinella will take their classes to the Museum in Stamford, Connecticut.

May 20th   Mr. Zillo's class will travel to Beardsley Park in Bridgeport.

May 26th   Mrs. Dabbo and Mrs. Byrne will take their classes to the White Memorial Institute in Litchfield, Connecticut.

June 3rd   Mrs. Lucas and Mrs. Shambreskis will take their classes to the Peabody Museum in New Haven, Connecticut.

June 5th   The kindergarten class will visit the Stamford Museum.

           Monday, May 25th

           Memorial Day

           Holiday

At left, the program cover (top) and list of performers (bottom) for a Chase School 'Stars of the Nineties' talent show in 1990.

Above, a page from a commemorative booklet of citywide festivities for Waterbury's Tercentennial celebration in 1974, depicting male teachers and staffers from Chase, who went without razors for a time to take part in a tercentennial event.

At right, the 'Chase School News' handout from May 1981, alerting students and their parents to a number of upcoming field trips, including visits to the Indian Institute in Washington, Conn., Beardsley Park in Bridgeport, the White Memorial in Litchfield and Peabody Museum in New Haven.

CLASS PHOTOS FROM THE 1980S/1990s

CHASE SCHOOL KDG PM

GRADE 1 MISS FAHY 1985

CHASE SCHOOL GRADE 4 MR GALLO 1992

CHASE ELEMENTARY SCHOOL MR PALERMO GRADE 2

SHOOTING FOR THE STARS WITH RICK

Chase School graduate and NASA astronaut Rick Mastracchio has returned to his former school a number of times to visit with students, to recount his adventures in space while helping to inspire city youngsters for their own future endeavors. Mastracchio, a member of the last class to complete eighth grade at Chase in 1974, has flown on three NASA Space Shuttle missions as a mission specialist, in addition to serving as a flight engineer on a Soyuz TMA-11M long-duration mission aboard the International Space Station.

A NASA suit now stands in the main office at Chase, to honor Rick's achievements and embolden students' ambitions.

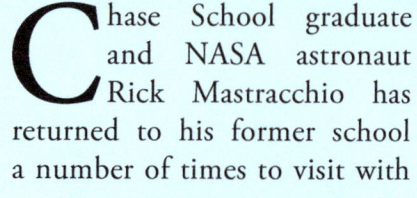

Photos contributed by H.S. Chase School

MORE VISITS FROM DIGNITARIES

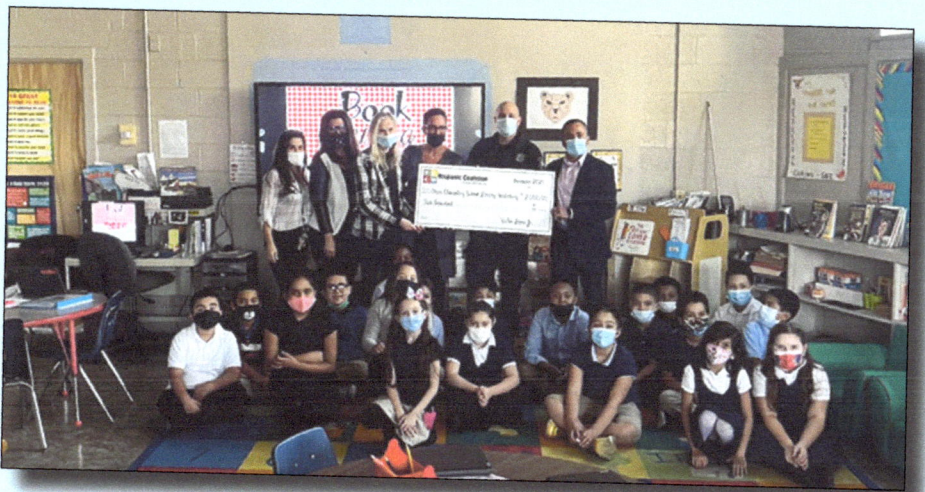

Photos contributed by
H.S. Chase School

Chase School has been honored to welcome a number of city and state officials and other dignitaries for visits, including:

■ Top left: Former Governor William O'Neill, who served from 1980 to 1991, speaks with students (Principal Joseph Skerritt is at far left).

■ Top right: State Sen. Joan Hartley and city officials present a check for the school library.

■ Bottom left: Superintendent Verna Ruffin presents a Smarter Balance school award to current principal Lori Kramarz-Eldridge.

■ Bottom right: Santa makes a stop (with Kaynor Tech's Honor Society) to bring gifts for Chase students.

55

LATEST DEVELOPMENTS AT H.S. CHASE

While H.S. Chase Elementary School has gone without a major renovation in the past half-century, the school has undergone some physical improvements over the years.

Among the most recent improvements is a new elevator at one end of the complex, constructed along with an accessible entrance on the Meriden Road side (shown in photo at left below) in 2019.

Recent years have also seen new windows installed at H.S. Chase and other grammar schools in Waterbury (examples in both photos below).

A number of new programs and activities for students are also among the latest developments at Chase, some of which are featured on the next page.

Contributed photos

Accessibility at Chase School has been improved with the addition of an elevator and new entrance (shown in photo at left). New windows (pictured at right) are also among the latest improvements at the school.

Photos contributed by
H.S. Chase School

Programs and activities recently introduced at H.S. Chase School include:

■ Connecticut's Kid Governor – a civics program for fifth graders designed by the Connecticut Democracy Center that focuses on government, elections and voting – offering schools the opportunity to enter a student candidate into a statewide election (featured in photos at right).

■ A Spanish holiday dance (seen in photo at top right) is one of a number of activities exemplifying the variety of offerings for Chase School's diverse student body.

■ The Stuck for a Buck fundraiser in 2022 for the Lymphoma and Leukemia Society – among the various efforts the school participates in – had Principal Lori Kramarz-Eldridge 'all tied up' for a good cause.

OTHER NOTABLE BEGINNINGS IN 1922

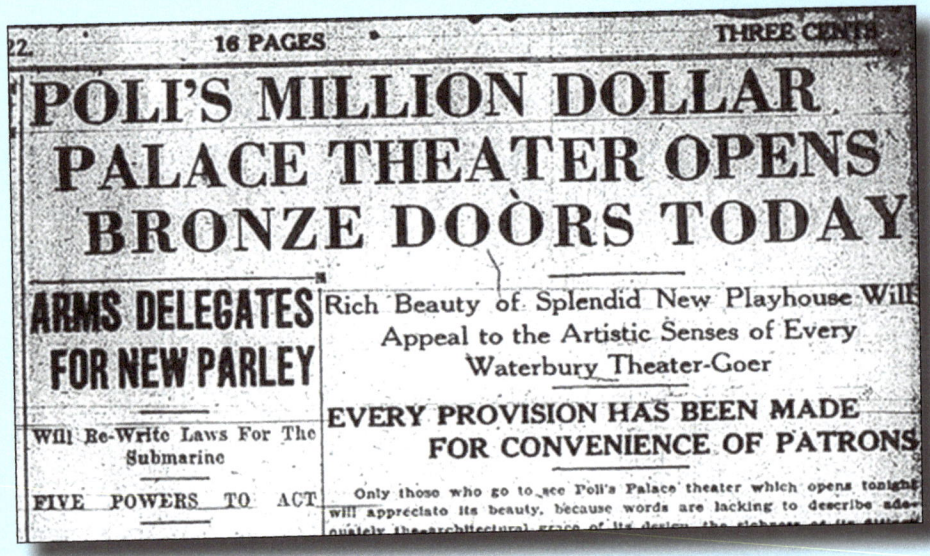

News of Poli's Palace opening in January 1922.

The reconstruction and renaming of H.S. Chase Elementary School was not the only noteworthy happening in Waterbury in 1922.

Here are some other notable beginnings from 100 years ago:

■ The first UNICO Club was founded in Waterbury in 1922, when Dr. Anthony P. Vastola and others of Italian heritage formed a club to foster civic and cultural development and serve the community. One hundred years later, the UNICO Club has grown to comprise 150 regional groups throughout the country, with more than 8,000 members involved. The group's name is the Italian word for "unique," or "one of a kind;" and UNICO has become an acronym that stands for Unity, Neighborliness, Integrity, Charity, and Opportunity.

■ One of Waterbury's prominent entertainment landmarks, the Palace Theater, was first opened 100 years ago. Famed New England theater impresario Sylvester Z. Poli invested $1 million of improvements and op-

A plaque commemorating the Unico Club's founding.

Contributed photo

Waterbury's Fire Station 2, on East Main Street.

ulent decor into an existing theater and opened Poli's Palace on January 28, 1922, with two presentations of George M. Cohen's "Mary." Presenting quality vaudeville and augmented picture presentations with the Palace Symphony Orchestra, the theater was quickly received as the city's finest performance venue and served as the center of Waterbury's active cultural scene.

■ Also in 1922, the Waterbury Clock Company purchased the bankrupt watch-making enterprise of Robert H. Ingersoll & Bros. and began focusing on producing smaller and smaller movements designed to fit on a person's wrist. In the following decade, the company designed one of the most iconic watches in U.S. history after obtaining a license to produce a watch featuring Mickey Mouse on its face. In the 1950s, it released an inexpensive and reliable wristwatch named the "Timex." The product eventually became such an important part of the company's business that the company changed its name to Timex in the 1960s.

■ Sacred Heart High School in Waterbury was the first Catholic high school in Connecticut, opening its doors to students on September 6, 1922. The private, Roman Catholic high school was originally established as an all-girls school, before becoming co-educational in 1938. In 1975, Sacred Heart moved into the former Waterbury Catholic High School building in downtown Waterbury, where it stood for 45 more years, before closing in 2021.

■ Dating to 1922, Fire Station 2 of the Waterbury Fire Department is home to Truck 3 and Engine 2. The station is located at 519 East Main Street.

■ One of the city's noted journalists, Sherman London, was born in 1922. His first job after graduating from Rider College in 1942 was at the former Waterbury Democrat, before he moved on to the Waterbury Republican – where he served as a political and legislative reporter, assistant managing editor, and then as the newspaper's editorial director for the last 20 years of his career. An advocate of freedom of information in Connecticut, London served as an FOI commissioner for a time. He served a term as president of the Connecticut Chapter of the Society of Professional Journalists, and was inducted into the Connecticut Journalism Hall of Fame in 2007.

Source: SHHS

Sacred Heart High School.

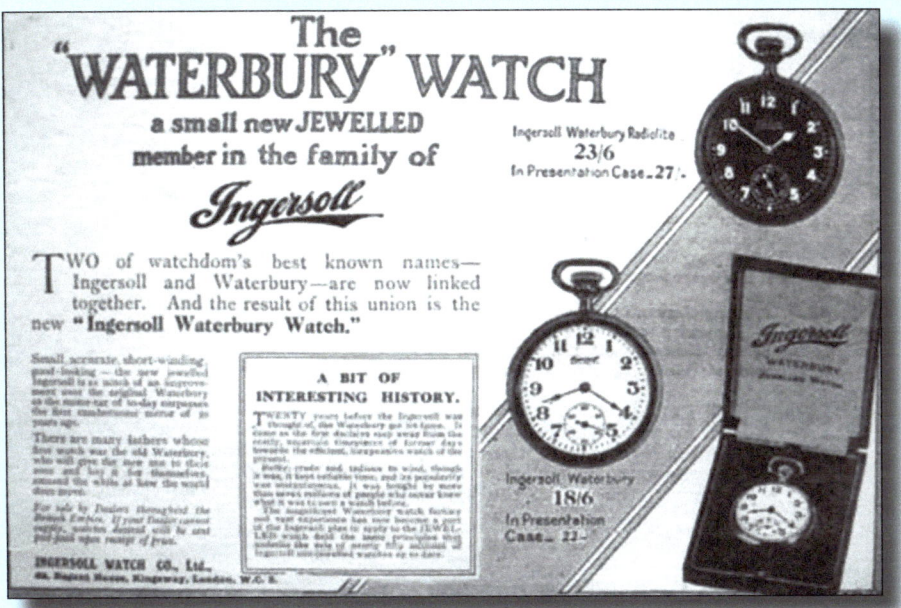

Source: Ingersoll Bros./ Waterbury Antique Clocks

An old advertisement/label for the Ingersoll/Waterbury watch.

REFERENCES/ WORKS CITED

Photos contributed by the Gottscho-Schleisner collection at the Library of Congress

Books:

Anderson, Joseph. "The Town And City of Waterbury, Connecticut, From The Aboriginal Period To The Year 1895." New Haven: The Price and Lee Company, 1896.

Pape, William J. "History Of Waterbury And The Naugatuck Valley (Connecticut)." Chicago, New York: The S.J. Clarke Publishing Company, 1918

Watkins, William H.; Sargent, Margaret S.; Maloney, Cornelius F.; The Mattatuck Historical Society. "Waterbury, 1674-1974: A Pictorial History." The Globe Pequot Press, 1974.

Thesis Project:

Iorio, Mary Lonergan. "An Historical Study Of Public Education In Waterbury, Connecticut." (Requirement for Master of Science degree from Southern Connecticut State College) 1968.

Others:

Waterbury Board of Education Annual Reports, (Waterbury, Connecticut); 1886 to 1928

Waterbury Hall of Fame, Silas Bronson Library (Waterbury, Connecticut), initiated in 1986.

Newspapers:

"Waterbury Democrat." (Waterbury, Connecticut)
"Waterbury Evening Democrat." (Waterbury, Connecticut)
"Waterbury Republican." (Waterbury, Connecticut)

CONTRIBUTORS

In addition to the sources listed on the page at left, a number of individuals have contributed materials, photographs or other information used in this book. They include research staffers at rhe Silas Bronson Library and the Mattatuck Museum, along with: Lori Anton-Ritch, Derek Guisto, Ray Sullivan, Arthur and Vera Jarjura, Jay Skerritt, Lou Martelli, Roxanne Russell, Debra Parry, Vincent Didominzio, Leslie Dempsey, Nancy Mattaboni, Gina Sciortino-Farrington, Victoria Bonacassio, Nancy Armour, Michele O'Connor Mark and Beth McHugh, Joan Thomas, Nancy White, Angelo Mazzeo, Erica Tutino, Sonja Selenica, and the Chase Centennial and East Enders Facebook groups.

Photos contributed by the Gottscho-Schleisner collection at the Library of Congress

Photo contributed by H.S. Chase School

The morning kindergarten class of Miss Mullaly and Mrs. Boucher at H.S. Chase for the 1970-71 school year. Michael Griffin, who composed this book, is pictured fourth from the right in the midde row.

ABOUT THE AUTHOR

This "Pictorial History of H.S. Chase Elementary School" was composed by Michael Griffin, who attended Chase from kindergarten through fifth grade.

In keeping with this book's format, at left is a photo of Michael's kindergarten class, taught by Miss Mullaly and Mrs. Boucher, from the 1970-71 school year.

Currently a copy desk editor with the Republican-American newspaper in Waterbury, Griffin is the author of "Hoop History: Fifty years of high school boys basketball in Waterbury" (cover shown at right).

More information on both books can be found at highburypress.com, where they are both available for purchase.

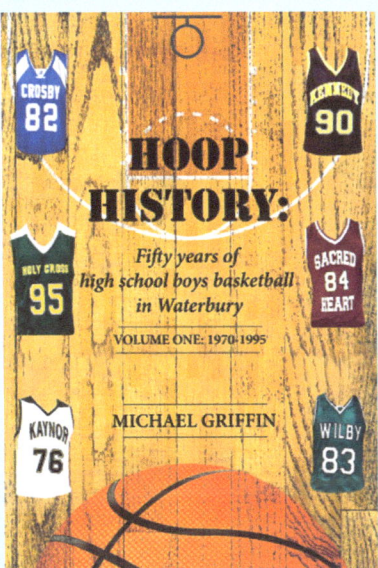

63